"God wants His people walking in freedom and victory. Rabbi Schneider is an overcomer who has learned from experience how to press in to God for his own deliverance and freedom, and who is called to teach others. Expect to be set free as you read this book!"

Rabbi Jonathan Bernis, president and CEO,
Jewish Voice Ministries International

"We are in a spiritual war. The apostle Paul says, 'The weapons of our warfare are . . . divinely powerful for the destruction of fortresses' (2 Corinthians 10:4). Rabbi Schneider unsheathes the weapons every believer must use to win our individual battles against demonic powers."

Pat Boone, entertainer and author

"I have known Rabbi Schneider for more than twenty years. I believe his new book, *Self-Deliverance*, will prove to be the right book at the right time. The Church is beginning to come into an understanding of not only what the Bible says but, more importantly, what the Bible emphasizes. Deliverance from demonic spirits remains very high on that list. Bravo!"

Scott T. Kelso, president,
Charismatic Leaders Fellowship

SELF-DELIVERANCE

How to Gain Victory OVER the Powers of Darkness

RABBI

K. A. SCHNEIDER

Chosen

a division of Baker Publishing Group

Minneapolis, Minnesota

Published by Chosen Books
11400 Hampshire Avenue South
Bloomington, Minnesota 55438
www.chosenbooks.com

Chosen Books is a division of
Baker Publishing Group, Grand Rapids, Michigan

Printed in the United States of America

Library of Congress Cataloging-in-Publication Data
Schneider, K. A. (Kirt Allan)
    Self-deliverance : how to gain victory over the powers of darkness /
Messianic Rabbi K.A. Schneider.
        pages cm
    Summary: "Rabbi Schneider shares the practical, biblical principles of self-deliverance, showing you how to break demonic strongholds and maintain your freedom"— Provided by publisher.
        ISBN 978-0-8007-9775-1 (pbk. : alk. paper)
    1. Spiritual warfare. I. Title.
    BV4509.5.S354 2015
    235′.4—dc23   2015005500

Cover design by Dan Pitts

15   16   17   18   19   20   21   7   6   5   4   3   2

This book is dedicated, with love and appreciation,
to the Freedom and Deliverance Ministry Team
that I have trained and raised up
at Lion of Judah World Outreach Center
in Toledo, Ohio.
I want to thank them for their hard work,
sacrifice and love as they continue
to minister freedom and deliverance
to those in need.

Contents

Introduction

Let me begin by telling you that many of the problems you and I deal with are coming from the realm of darkness and are demonic.

If you find this hard to believe, you are not alone.

The topic of demons is almost foreign in the Western Church. While Scripture looks squarely at the reality of demonic bondage, many people who love Jesus shy away from it. It seems easier—and somehow safer—to think that demonic effects are the result of natural phenomena or perhaps a medical issue. Or they conclude that maybe demons do affect some people, but this must be a rarity, occurring in only extreme cases, as in the movie *The Exorcist*.

Whatever way they choose to bypass the subject, many of God's people are letting wrong paradigms keep them from the truth. They never consider that the Bible is specific about this: Demons are a problem for all of us. And unless we come to grips with the fact that we are dealing with spirits—spirits that plague us with false perceptions of reality, false perceptions of God, false perceptions of life, false perceptions of ourselves—unless we realize that these false perceptions are delusions from the realm of darkness to destroy us and to mock God, we are never going to get free.

The Lord wants us to have spiritual discernment about what is happening in our own lives and the lives of those around us. He wants to show us the nature of this battle and equip us so that we can defeat Satan and put him under our feet.

Think for a moment about how much of Jesus' ministry dealt with casting out demons. From the very beginning, Jesus dealt with people who had problems with demons. Matthew 4:23–24 states this specifically:

> Jesus was going throughout all of Galilee, teaching in their synagogues and proclaiming the gospel of the kingdom. . . . [They] brought to Him . . . demoniacs . . . and He healed them.

Matthew 8:16 says: "When evening came, they brought to Him many who were demon-possessed; and He cast out the spirits with a word."

How many? *Many* who were demon-possessed.

Not only did Jesus Himself set people free, but He also taught His disciples to deliver people who had been snared by these evil spiritual beings: "He appointed twelve, so that they would be with Him and that He could send them out to preach and to have authority to cast out the demons" (Mark 3:14–15).

He then appointed seventy others to go out and proclaim the Good News, and they returned saying, "Lord, even the demons are subject to us in Your name" (Luke 10:17).

Casting out demons was a pillar in the ministry Jesus established. Before His ascension into heaven, Jesus spoke these parting words to His disciples, known as the Great Commission: "Go into all the world and preach the gospel to all creation. . . . These signs will accompany those who have believed: in My name they will cast out demons" (Mark 16:15, 17).

The question to us, then, is this: Should the call on Jesus' Church today be any different from the call on His followers when He walked the earth? He wants us to preach, to share the Gospel, to heal—but He *also* wants us to use the authority He has given us to cast out demons. Demons are for real. Jesus does not want us to be destroyed by these spiritual beings.

Maybe you picked up this book because you sense that something is happening around you in the spirit realm, but you are not exactly sure what it is. Or perhaps you are well aware that demons are plaguing your life, and it seems as if you cannot escape the harassment.

I want to encourage you that help is available for you. You can live in freedom from demonic bondage. And you do not have to wait for somebody else to deliver you. You can free yourself.

Throughout this book we will learn the principles from Scripture that teach us how to drive demons out of our lives. Not only is "self-deliverance" possible for every believer, it is a necessary and important part of our walk in Yeshua.

How does this happen?

In order to gain victory over evil spirits, we need to confront them, to take authority over them and to replace their lies with truth. You will learn how to do this. We will explore every aspect of the process of self-deliverance.

Not only will you discover that you are winning the battle against demonic spirits, but you will find that taking hold of these simple truths affects the way you experience the presence of God. As you move into His freedom, you will begin to notice a change in the atmosphere that surrounds you. You will begin literally to see darkness dissipate. And you will find yourself being surrounded by peace and clarity that you have not known before.

In order to act on a word, we must first receive it. Until we resolve to combat the demons afflicting us, we will never enter into the happiness we are looking for. It is just that simple. We must fight, and we must overcome. There is really no other way to fullness of life in Messiah Jesus.

Remember that Jesus' first act after being declared the Lamb of God was to go into the wilderness and defeat the devil. *Then He emerged in the power of the Spirit.*

Do you think this applies to our lives today? I do. Let's get started.

1

The Battle Begins

Deliverance was a significant part of Jesus' ministry. Everywhere He went—down dusty roads, in homes, in synagogues—He encountered people who were tormented and oppressed by evil spirits. And because He loved the people, He spoke a word and drove the demons out.

In the three years that Jesus ministered on the earth, in fact, fully one-third of His teaching involved deliverance. Jesus set people free who had been snared by demons, and He instructed His disciples to do the same. We can assume that demonic bondage was a big deal for Him since He focused so much of His life's work on it.

So I want to ask you a question. Clearly, demons were rampant on earth during the time of Jesus. Where, then, did all the demons go?

If while on earth Yeshua taught His disciples to deal with spirits that were coming from the realm of darkness, does it follow that He simply removed those spirits when He ascended to heaven? Are they no longer tormenting people? Are our problems with demons over?

No, the same demons that Jesus dealt with two thousand years ago are present, in like kind, today. Demons did not cease to exist after Jesus left the world. They are still here. I believe that if He were walking on earth today, He would continue to set many of us free from spirits that we do not even realize are plaguing us.

You have a real enemy; you have a real need to defend yourself.

If we believe the Word of God, we have to believe that much of the pressure on our lives comes from powers of darkness that surround us and are operating in our world. If we want to walk in the apostolic calling of the Church, we must recognize that people are in bondage and need to be set free. *We* need to be set free.

Now this is nothing to be afraid of. Jesus has prepared the way through His victory at the cross. We can defend ourselves; we have everything we need to deliver ourselves from demons!

A few years ago I realized that a number of people in the congregation that I pastor were struggling with demons. To help them be set free, I trained a team to minister deliverance. Almost without exception, the people who were ministered to expressed a sense of freedom and lightness afterward.

But two problems began to surface. First, there were so many people asking for help that the team was booked a year in advance. I felt burdened by this. These people needed help *now*, and they had to wait many months before we could minister to them. The second problem was that many of them who received deliverance were soon plagued by evil spirits again. They were not able to stay on the path of freedom.

As I took this matter to prayer, the Lord led me to start teaching self-deliverance. This solved both problems. People no longer had to wait for someone else to help them. They understood the battle and had the appropriate weapons to deal with the problem themselves. And since they were now trained and equipped, they could continue to protect themselves every time the enemy stalked them.

There is really no way to walk in the freedom that the Lord desires for us if we cannot fight for ourselves. Think of this analogy: Suppose you are a kid in school being picked on by a bully. Your big brother or dad might confront the bully, and this will gain you some temporary relief. But, chances are, as soon as your brother or dad is not around, the bully is going to return and take your lunch money or beat you up or do whatever he wants to do. The only way to get free and remain free from the bully's torment is to stand up to the bully *yourself*.

We do not have to wait for someone to come help us, and we do not have to live in torment and demonic oppression. But we do have to understand that we are in a fight and that we need certain weapons to defend ourselves.

The Church's Usual Stance

Scripture explains that this fight is not against "flesh and blood, but against the rulers, against the powers, against the world forces of this darkness, against the spiritual forces of wickedness in the heavenly places" (Ephesians

6:12). Yet have you noticed that many believers who say *amen* to this truth cover their ears and run from any discussion about demons? Fear and demonic oppression are only going to intensify as we move deeper into the end-time darkness of this world.

The Church sometimes skirts her own doctrines regarding deliverance.

If we are honest, we have to admit that the Church today is ill-equipped to deal with the struggle against demons. Why is this so? In the first place, there is not a great deal being taught about demonic activity.

How many of us, who have been in church for years, who are worshiping Jesus, who are singing the love songs and who are talking about the beautiful attributes of God, are also being taught extensively about facing the devil? We have too often put our heads into the ground when it comes to understanding the nature of the battle we are in. We say we are in agreement with the doctrines that Scripture teaches, but there is a big gap between what we believe intellectually and what we actually believe in our hearts.

Rather than grasp the fact that our true enemy comes from the spiritual realm, we take out our frustration on people and circumstances. We have minimal ability to see past the material world, so we stay trapped in it. And because we are focused on what we see with our eyes, we are continually being deceived and beaten up by the devil. We are not experiencing the freedom, the peace and the clarity of heart and mind that are ours in Christ Jesus.

Our discomfort with this subject leads to a second reason that the Church is weak in her struggle against demons. We have drifted into the theology that, even supposing demons are real, they cannot afflict a *Christian*. We are more comfortable assuming that they have influence only on people who do not know the Lord, who are not true believers.

"I'm a Christian," we say with conviction. "I'm immune to all this. Demons can't touch me."

Scripture, however, negates this idea, telling us to stay on the alert: "Your adversary, the devil, prowls around like a roaring lion, seeking someone to devour" (1 Peter 5:8). Whose adversary? *Your adversary!*

Peter is speaking to the Church. This letter was not written to people who were not saved. And notice that Ephesians 6:12 states that *our* struggle is not against flesh and blood but against spiritual forces of darkness. Paul is not describing the struggle of unbelievers or reprobates. He is talking about the struggle of God's people. *Our* struggle. Yours and mine!

Squatters in the Temple

The story of Yeshua cleansing the Temple gives us further insight into the reality that demons are a problem for believers. When He was on earth and people wanted to come and fellowship with God, they went to the Temple in Jerusalem. Jesus did much of His ministry there.

On one particular day near the time of the Passover, Jesus went into the Temple and saw moneychangers at work. Look at John's description of what happened.

> He found in the temple those who were selling oxen and sheep and doves, and the money changers seated at their tables. And He made a scourge of cords, and drove them all out of the temple, with the sheep and the oxen; and

He poured out the coins of the money changers and over-turned their tables; and to those who were selling the doves He said, "Take these things away; stop making My Father's house a place of business."

John 2:14–16

Now the Temple was God's territory and His property, but intruders—greedy, demonically driven money-changers—had moved in and set up shop. They had to be driven out. I think this serves as a good pattern for us as we engage in spiritual warfare.

The Bible says that we are temples of the living and holy God (see 1 Corinthians 3:16). Just as demons intruded into God's sacred Temple in ancient Israel through the moneychangers, so demons can intrude into our temples. And when they do, they seek to bring us into bondage, entrap us in fear, limit our awareness of Jesus' presence and keep us from experiencing the fullness of our inheritance in our relationship with God.

Be assured, though, that even if demons do set up camp in believers' hearts and minds, they cannot possess us. The word *possession*, which is often used when demons are spoken of, implies ownership. Satan can never own us. We have been bought by the blood of the Lamb. After Jesus was crucified, ascended into heaven and was seated at the right hand of God, the Holy Spirit came. Through the Holy Spirit, Jesus is now living in the hearts of all who receive Him as Lord and Savior. Jesus owns us. We are the Church and the Bride of Jesus.

But demons can occupy our space *illegally,* just as the moneychangers did at the Temple, and when they do they will try to keep us from ejecting them.

The Lord showed me something about this concept in a vivid dream He gave me. In this dream, I was living in a tiny, dilapidated house that was almost falling apart. As you can imagine, I did not have a good feeling living in that house.

Now, right next door to this run-down house was another house. This second house was gorgeous. It was brand new. It was modern. It was clean. It was big. It was beautiful—and it was *my* house. I was the owner. But I was not living in the nice house; I was living in the broken-down house.

Why was I not living in the nice house that I owned? Because it was inhabited by squatters. They had human form, but they were demonically energized, violent and hateful.

What about being "possessed" by evil spirits? Can that happen?

I was afraid to take possession of the house because they were threatening me, telling me what they would do to me if I tried. I was certain that if I set foot in the house they would attack, and God knows what they would do. So I was being tormented, letting other people take what was mine, afraid even to go inside.

Eventually, as the dream progressed, I got up enough courage. I decided that I was not going to be afraid and tormented and let them have my house. It was no longer an option. I was going to have to face those demons and drive them out.

So I went around to the side door and waited for the chief demon. When he came out, I grabbed him by the collar, threw him to the ground and began punching him in the face.

At first it seemed as though nothing was happening. He acted as though I was having no effect on him at all. My punches did not seem to be making even the smallest dent.

But you know what? I was so focused on defeating this demon that I just kept pounding and pounding. All of a sudden, I heard a sound like *psssshhhh*, as the air went out from him. He evaporated, and was gone.

There are other aspects of this dream that we will get into later, but the point I want to make now is this: Demons do not possess believers, but they can become squatters, just as those squatters in my dream were occupying my house. In the next chapter we will learn some of the ways that demons take up residence in our lives, but basically, like the moneychangers in the Temple, Satan gets hold of some part of us and lodges himself into a space that is not his. God has something so much nicer for us, just as the Lord showed me in the dream. He had a much nicer house for me to live in. If we become trapped in fear, in worry, in wrong thoughts, we will never enjoy what God has provided for us.

Demons are looking for the weak, the vulnerable, those who do not know how to defend themselves. Furthermore, demons will not leave their habitations simply because their consciences begin to convict them. They will not wake up one day and realize they did not pay for the space they are living in, so they probably should leave. No, they have to be confronted with the truth about Yeshua's identity and our identity in Him, and commanded to go. Self-deliverance is applying the means that God gives us to drive out the demons that are invading our space and keeping us in bondage.

Our Warrior King

The Bible says that He who raised Jesus from the dead dwells in our mortal bodies. The Spirit of the living God actually lives within us. In all things, we rely on Him and trust Him to release life to our mortal flesh. This does not mean, however, that we are immune to spiritual attack any more than we are immune to physical attack. Might a believer catch a cold or get an infection? Yes, this happens, even though we look to Jesus for our physical health. Well, just so, we will be attacked by our spiritual enemy even though we look to Jesus for our spiritual health.

It is important to get this foundational understanding as we move into the principles of self-deliverance: Our God is a God of war. We have an enemy, and God wants to train and equip His people to fight.

In the Hebrew Bible, the concept of warfare was generalized in the natural realm in a well-known story. When the children of Israel were ready to enter their Promised Land, they had to *drive out* the Amorites, the Hittites, the Jebusites, the Canaanites and all the other "ites" in order to take possession.

The Lord spoke to His people and said, "I will fix your boundary from the Red Sea to the sea of the Philistines, and from the wilderness to the River Euphrates; for I will deliver the inhabitants of the land into your hand, and *you will drive them out* before you" (Exodus 23:31, emphasis added).

This story from Scripture is a prophetic shadow of how we begin to enter into the fullness of the freedom that we have inherited in Jesus. Just as the Israelites had to drive out her enemies in the physical realm, so we have to drive out our enemies in the spiritual realm. You might consider someone at work to be your enemy, but he is not really the basis of your struggle. Your struggle is in the realm of the heavenly.

In Numbers 32:21, we see the Israelites engaged in actual conflict: "All of you armed men cross over the Jordan before the LORD until He has driven His enemies out from before Him." I like this concept of being armed as we apply it to our spiritual battle. We will discuss the power and authority that are ours in Jesus in later chapters, but understand for now that the Church must engage in the battle.

And we must keep on fighting. We do not win a skirmish and then sit back and do nothing when the enemy returns. If we are going to prevail in Jesus' name, we must know how to drive the enemy out—and be ready to fight again.

If you sense that demonic activity is harassing you, you do not need to run from reality. The truth is uncomfortable sometimes, but we cannot pursue freedom without also pursuing the truth. Jesus said, "If you *continue* in My word, then you are truly disciples of Mine; and you will know the truth, and the truth will make you free" (John 8:31–32, emphasis added). We continue to fight, and Jesus leads us into greater and greater freedom.

The Real Mr. Nice Guy

In one of David's psalms of deliverance, he wrote about the importance of being trained and armed: "[God] trains my hands for battle, so that my arms can bend a bow of bronze" (2 Samuel 22:35). In Psalm 144:1, he said: "Blessed be the LORD, my rock, who trains my hands for war, and my fingers for battle." This man after God's own heart was not only a shepherd and a musician but also a warrior. David related to God as a father who trained him for warfare.

What does that mean for us? A lot of times the Church seems to think that following Jesus is equivalent to being "nice." Now, believers should by their very nature have a quality that the world perhaps calls "niceness," but we also need to know how to enter the battle zone and expect victory.

Jesus did. Jesus referred to Himself as "the descendant of David" (Revelation 22:16); we see in His personality the same warrior trait that David exemplified.

When it comes to the battle with evil, it is time to rethink Jesus' words about "turning the other cheek."

Jesus was aggressive against darkness in any form. We saw that He drove the moneychangers out of the Temple with a whip. He also turned around to Peter, looked him in the eye and said, "Get behind Me, Satan!" In one discourse alone He called the scribes and Pharisees "hypocrites," "son[s] of hell," "fools," "whitewashed tombs . . . full of dead men's bones" and a "brood of vipers" (see Matthew 23) as He aggressively opposed darkness.

We need to rethink our one-dimensional perception of Yeshua as just a nice guy. The Jesus who always turned the other cheek. The Jesus who was born in a lowly stable. These things are true of the Prince of Peace, but they do not express the full dimension of who Jesus really is. He is also a warrior: He is the one coming back riding a horse, with a sword protruding from His mouth.

> And I saw heaven opened, and behold, a white horse, and He who sat on it is called Faithful and True, and in

righteousness He judges and wages war. His eyes are a flame of fire, and on His head are many diadems; and He has a name written on Him which no one knows except Himself. He is clothed with a robe dipped in blood, and His name is called The Word of God. And the armies which are in heaven, clothed in fine linen, white and clean, were following Him on white horses. From His mouth comes a sharp sword, so that with it He may strike down the nations, and He will rule them with a rod of iron; and He treads the wine press of the fierce wrath of God, the Almighty. And on His robe and on His thigh He has a name written, "King of kings, and Lord of lords."

Revelation 19:11–16

This Mr. Nice Guy is coming back from heaven to deal out retribution upon those who do not know God. If we are going to embrace His offer of victory, then we need to take the concept of spiritual warfare seriously. This is part of walking with Jesus.

When we understand that there is an extensive demonic problem for those of us living on planet earth, we lay a foundation from the Word of God on which to stand and fight. Like our warrior King Jesus, we can dislodge these evil spirits and drive them out. The shackles of darkness will fall.

In the next chapters we begin our training for self-deliverance by understanding how demons gain access into our lives in the first place, and then we will close and lock those doors.

2

How Demons Gain Access

Randy felt terrible. He had screamed at his wife again and saw the tears welling up in her eyes. Why did anger sweep over him like that? He remembered from his childhood listening to his grandfather's voice berating his grandmother. And there were uncles whose tempers flared. Now he was sick to realize he sounded just like them. . . .

Melissa woke with a splitting headache. She made her way slowly to the kitchen, embarrassed to see yet another empty bottle on the table. Everything was just so stressful right now, that was all. As the bottle slipped into the trash can with a *clunk*, Melissa promised God that tonight would be different. . . .

Trevor closed his eyes and lay back on the sofa. This was not fair—being fired after twelve years. So what if he had trouble getting along with people. He was not the only person at the dealership with an attitude. His father's words came back to him, pounding in his head: *You are so stupid. What's the matter with you?...*

If these or any one of a thousand related scenarios sounds familiar, it is because demons will take advantage of every opportunity to destroy your life. They know your weak places—the actual chinks in your armor that serve as an open door. They know better than you do where you are vulnerable to sin, where you are afraid. They know how to slip through an opening and take up residence.

Demons know more about you than you realize— and they will use it against you.

They also know that your position in Jesus can send them running. They are hoping that you will not walk in freedom— but we are going to learn how to do precisely that. I am going to show you how to face demons and drive them and their evil effects out.

The first step of self-deliverance is to understand *how* demons get in. In a moment we will look at the three main entry points: generational patterns, personal sin and wounding from the outside. Then we will learn how to shut these points of access, which is our battle plan for the chapter that follows.

Remember, as we go along, to pray for revelation of the fact that this really is a spiritual battle. We say it is a spiritual battle, we believe it is a spiritual battle, but we seem to have little insight or revelation of how God wants to train us for this type of war. I know this has been the case for me. I have been praying for years that God will give me greater clarity and understanding so that I will be able to see in the Spirit and not act according to the flesh. We will never beat the devil and his demons by warring in the flesh.

I want to encourage you to make this a focal point of your prayer dialogue with God as well. Like Paul, we want to pray to Yeshua HaMashiach, which is Hebrew for "Jesus, the Anointed One," that He will open the eyes of our hearts to see in the Spirit that our fight is spiritual. We want to come to the place where we can see as Jesus sees.

What Are Demons?

Every person who is alive is struggling against the darkness that is operating in our world. When we speak about darkness, we might imagine a general sense of the power or force of evil. But when we speak about demons, we are talking about actual creatures. These dark beings are fallen angels, servants of Satan that were cast out of heaven with him.

> Then another sign appeared in heaven: and behold, a great red dragon having seven heads and ten horns, and on his heads were seven diadems. And his tail swept away a third of the stars of heaven and threw them to the earth. . . . And the great dragon was thrown down, the serpent of old who is called the devil and Satan, who deceives the whole world; he was thrown down to the earth, and his angels were thrown down with him.
>
> Revelation 12:3–4, 9

Demons have intellect; they have motives; they have personalities. Generally, their personalities exhibit the types of sins that we see here on earth. In other words, individual demons show characteristics of anger, lust, thievery, self-loathing, sarcasm and on and on. These dark angels are the enemies of our souls. Like Satan, they hate all of humanity because we have been created in God's image.

When we see pride and envy and all manner of evil around us—and sometimes directed at us—we need to understand the source of these things and who the enemy really is.

Which Demons Target Us?

There are things we do, as well as things that are done to us, that can draw demons to us. If we have not closed the doors of access, they can come in and attach themselves to us. The story of Jesus healing the demoniacs in the book of Matthew shows how demons are drawn to and seek to express themselves through flesh and blood.

> When He came to the other side into the country of the Gadarenes, two men who were demon-possessed met Him as they were coming out of the tombs. They were so extremely violent that no one could pass by that way. And they cried out, saying, "What business do we have with each other, Son of God? Have You come here to torment us before the time?"
>
> Now there was a herd of many swine feeding at a distance from them. The demons began to entreat Him, saying, "If You are going to cast us out, send us into the herd of swine."
>
> Matthew 8:28–31

Though demons can inhabit animals, they want primarily to link themselves to human beings. Demons can attach themselves to the mind or any part of the body. They generally attack and gain entrance through our thoughts.

Which demons do we attract? Any sinful behavior opens the door for demons of that type to gain entrance and lodge themselves within us.

Say that a woman has a problem with gossip. She does not control her tongue and yields to this sin more and more easily. Her behavior is going to catch the attention of a demon who feeds on gossip. Now she has a bigger problem to overcome.

Or say a man steps outside of God's boundary of marriage in the area of his sexuality. He yields to the lower nature and falls into adultery. Now he has taken a natural and beautiful gift that God has provided and turned it into an act of selfishness that

Demons seek flesh-and-blood bodies to inhabit.

attracts demons of lust and perversion. His mind and body will be energized by the demons that attach themselves to him.

Or take something good like food. There is obviously nothing wrong with enjoying food. God is a God of pleasure. He created tongues and taste buds. This is part of His goodness. But if we allow ourselves to be overcome by the flesh and fall into gluttony, we are going to attract demons whose personalities feed on gluttony. They will wrap themselves around our thinking and dominate our actions. This leads only to despair.

Points of Entry

Scripture tells us that God offers us protective spiritual armor. As believers who love Jesus, we might assume that our armor is securely locked into place. How, then, can demons find a way through? In the case of open sin, the inroad seems obvious. But what if we are sincerely living in the love and charity of Jesus, confessing our wrongs and trying to do right? How do they still get in?

Here are the three main areas of entry.

First, demonic attachment to our lives might not have anything to do with us at all, but everything to do with our family histories. The iniquities of our ancestors, called "generational sins," can open the door for demons. These patterns of sin and rebellion can appear in our families and our own lives in any number of ways—immorality, depression, anxiety, chronic sickness.

Second, as we might assume, any decision we make to indulge in sin opens the door to demons. Even if this sinful behavior occurred before we knew Jesus, and even if we have repented, we sometimes continue to struggle with demons that attached at that time.

And, third, wounds inflicted on us by others can leave us open and vulnerable.

These access points can give demons the opportunity they seek in order to enter into our lives. Even if demons came before we accepted Jesus as Lord, and even though demons must bow to His name, they often will stubbornly remain until told to leave.

Let's look more closely at these three access points. Again, we will deal with the effects of these openings in the next chapter.

Generational Patterns

If you go to a doctor for a checkup, and it is your initial visit, you will likely be given a health questionnaire to fill out. The doctor wants to know what diseases, illnesses and vulnerabilities exist in your family history. Did your parents have diabetes? Has anyone had a heart attack? Is there a history of high blood pressure?

Doctors do this because they know the propensity for these physical weaknesses to be passed on through the generations, right?

Well, the same phenomenon is true in the realm of the spirit. If someone in your family opened the door to the demonic through an iniquity, then demons can enter through that opening and travel down the family line. Even if you have never taken part in the particular sin that let the demons in, they can affect you and your children.

This explains why we sometimes struggle in certain areas and cannot break free, or our children cannot break free, and we have no clue why. We simply cannot figure out if we did something to allow these things or to cause these things to happen.

In many cases we are struggling with demonic personalities that have been living in our families for generations. These are also called "familiar spirits." They seem familiar, like an unquestioned part of the family line, because they have been within the genealogy for years.

Typical examples are spirits of unforgiveness, resentment, poverty, inferiority, judgment, condemnation, adultery, divorce, alcoholism, lust, lying, hate, anger, selfishness, doubt. Almost any type of demon can enter this way. Ask God to show you if there are any spirits that have been in the generational history of your family that might be affecting you. Even if it sounds implausible, listen to what the Holy Spirit might be telling you. There could be sins in your family line that you are unaware of.

We are taught this concept of generational sin in the Word of God—from the Torah. These words below are part of the Ten Commandments:

> "You shall not make for yourself an idol, or any likeness of what is in heaven above or on the earth beneath or in the water under the earth. You shall not worship them or serve them; for I, the LORD your God, am a jealous God, visiting the iniquity of the fathers on the children, on the third and the fourth generations of those who hate Me, but showing lovingkindness to thousands, to those who love Me and keep My commandments."
>
> Exodus 20:4–6

These words that highlight generational curses and blessings were not given to the children of Israel as just an interesting addendum to the second Commandment; God later affirmed them to Moses.

In this remarkable story, Moses came down from Mount Sinai, the two tablets inscribed with the Ten Commandments in his arms, and saw that the Israelites had turned from God to worship a golden calf. He was so angry he "threw the tablets from his hands and shattered them at the foot of the mountain" (Exodus 32:19).

Your past generations can leave you vulnerable to demonic attack.

After dealing severely with this terrible sin in the camp, Moses entered into a dialogue with God and wound up asking God to show him His glory. God agreed, saying, "I Myself will make all My goodness pass before you," and then He added, "and [I] will proclaim the name of the LORD before you" (Exodus 33:19).

God then instructed Moses to cut two more stone tablets to replace the ones he had broken. Early in the morning, Moses took the new tablets up the mountain and called upon the name of the Lord. Once Moses was safely hidden in the cleft of a rock, the Lord passed by in front of him proclaiming:

> "The LORD, the LORD God, compassionate and gracious, slow to anger, and abounding in lovingkindness and truth; who keeps lovingkindness for thousands, who forgives iniquity, transgression and sin; yet He will by no means leave the guilty unpunished, *visiting the iniquity of fathers on the children and on the grandchildren to the third and fourth generations.*"
>
> Exodus 34:6–7, emphasis added

Scripture says that at this revelation of God's identity, "Moses made haste to bow low toward the earth and worship" (verse 8). Within God's perfectly balanced character of mercy and justice, He reveals to us that the decisions of our generations past affect us today and can lie at the root of problems we are presently experiencing.

But what if the sin was many generations back? Can it still affect us? The answer is usually yes. The struggle with demons lives on beyond the third or fourth generation because somewhere along the way, someone gave in to the particular sin that the family struggles with, and the cycle was renewed for another three or four generations. This is how demons travel down a family line.

This concept of generational consequences is also referred to in the New Testament. When Jesus and His disciples approached the man who was blind from birth, the disciples asked Jesus to tell them whose sin had caused this malady: Was it the man himself who had sinned or his parents?

In that instance, Jesus answered that it was neither, that the man's condition was a special purpose for the glory of God—and healed him. But we see that the disciples held the biblical view of the spiritual phenomenon that God revealed in Exodus: that grievous iniquities against God open the way for demons to afflict families for generations. They asked, "Who sinned, this man or his parents?"

Even with scriptural evidence, a lot of believers think that generational curses could not apply to them. They explain that they are freed from all curses because Jesus canceled curses at the cross.

Yes—praise God!—Jesus' shed blood purchased freedom for us. It is true that we are not under a curse in Jesus. This does not mean that we discount the reality of curses, but rather that we now have authority over them in His name and can break them off. This includes any power that is at work in our lives due to the sins of generations past.

Remember that Jesus cast out demons and taught His disciples to do the same. Full deliverance does not happen automatically because we are saved. We have to stand against evil in warfare when it comes against us. We participate in the process of victory by taking hold of all that Jesus has won for us.

Sometimes people find generational sin hard to accept simply because they cannot imagine their ancestors doing anything bad enough to warrant demonic habitation. This is naïveté, ignorance and pride, and it can block the way to freedom.

The idea of generational sin actually helps explain a perplexing comment that Jesus made. Look at Luke 14:26. Jesus said: "If anyone comes to Me, and does not hate his own father and mother and wife and children and brothers and sisters, yes, and even his own life, he cannot be My disciple." What does this mean, that a man must hate his own father and mother in order to be Jesus' disciple? It sounds unloving!

Why did Jesus say that? Because He wanted His followers to understand that if they did not relinquish every attachment, even those primary generational relationships, to become bonded to Him, they would continue to struggle in some area of their lives.

No matter how good our parents were, no matter how good our grandparents were and no matter how good great-great-great-grandma and grandpa were, they were human and subject to the frailties of human nature. If we want to be successful at self-deliverance, we need to recognize that actions in our families' generations could be keeping us in bondage to demons. Unless we are willing to look at our relationships and repudiate anything in them that hinders our walk with Jesus, we can never approach the fullness of freedom that He has for us.

Now, this certainly does not mean that we no longer love or honor those close to us. Think of it like a diamond; there are different facets of the same truth. We love our parents, we honor our parents; but at the same time we deal with demonic strongholds that might have entered through them into the family line.

If you grew up with a mom or a dad who was covered by a dark spirit such as anxiety, nervousness, depression, demonic lust or inferiority, if some pattern of bondage is part of your family history, it is imperative to remove it. Praise God, there is nothing to fear! In fact, this knowledge can help you identify the particular demons you might be facing. Begin to look for patterns in your family—alcoholism, early deaths, accidents, anger, miscarriages, broken relationships—whatever it might be. Write them down and keep the list.

Personal Sin

The next significant way that evil spirits gain access is through personal sin. Even if we feel helpless and hope that God will understand when we sin, we open the door for demons.

Sometimes it is our participation in one regrettable sinful action that gives demons the green light to harass us. Many times, though, the openings they use come from behavior that starts out within parameters that God allows.

Let's take the example of alcohol. Personally I do not think there is anything wrong with enjoying a drink. But if the enjoyment of alcohol starts to move outside of appropriate boundaries, then it can become something that is demonically controlled. I felt that very thing happening to me.

I enjoy a social drink now and then. I go to a restaurant. I have a glass of wine or a drink. I enjoy it. I never felt that I had a problem with it. But at one point in my life I started to discern a spirit of alcoholism coming toward me. I sensed that this spirit wanted to turn me into a drunk. My social drinking was within appropriate bounds, but I sensed that Satan was on the perimeter wanting to draw me into a spirit of alcoholism.

So I dealt with it by choosing to abstain from all alcohol for a year. After a time, the Holy Spirit showed me that the power coming against me was broken off of me, and that I could again enjoy a social drink without its becoming a problem.

People can open themselves to demonic consequences, whether they sin knowingly or unknowingly.

That is just an example of how something can shift from appropriate enjoyment to behavior that is satanically driven. I am grateful that the Lord gave me that discernment. But if I had failed to see the warning and to understand that I was moving into danger, I would have been responsible for the outcome.

Whether we sin willfully or "innocently," we remove ourselves from God's covering and open ourselves to demons. We are no longer in a place of protection; we enter into the realm of spiritual darkness through our sin, and demons will attach themselves to our lives.

This is really serious. This should make us afraid to sin. Proverbs 9:10 says: "The fear of the LORD is the beginning of wisdom." I think part of fearing the Lord is recognizing the consequences of not obeying Him. It does not mean that God's love for us changes, but that there are repercussions for us and our families.

Suppose there is a sexual demon looking for someone to inhabit. Then suppose a young man decides to take "one quick look" at pornography. That young man has now opened his "eye gates" wide for any demon who is oriented toward sexual perversion. And not just the young man. The demons have now gained entrance to his whole family. I have seen instances of parents opening the door to sexual demons who then began tormenting their children.

Some years ago a young family was part of our congregation. I was visiting them in their home and began chatting with the children. When they mentioned that they liked to watch television, I asked what their favorite shows were.

One of the children said *The Walking Dead*. The other one said *The Vampire Diaries*.

The parents of these children were attending church, but they were not making decisions that would help keep their family from being defiled. Neither were they teaching their children about the danger of mixing their lives with the pleasures of the world. In consequence, they were letting the guard down for the whole family. It was not long after this conversation that significant darkness manifested in their lives.

Let's not be like those who "knew God . . . [but] became futile in their speculations, and their foolish heart was darkened" (Romans 1:21). The Lord says that His people are destroyed for lack of knowledge (see Hosea 4:6). Begin to think about areas in your life in which you might be sensing demonic activity due to sin, and write them down as they come to you.

Remember, there is no fear in knowing the truth. Fear is one of the biggest areas that Satan uses to keep people in darkness and bondage. It is an agreement with the lie that God is not concerned with our particular needs or not powerful enough to help us.

He is "the way, and the truth, and the life" (John 14:6). There is no aspect of darkness that He has not overcome through His cross, and no valley of sin so deep that He cannot show us the way out.

Wounding from Others

The third primary way that demons gain access to us is through wounds that others inflict on us—or, more particularly, our negative response to those wounds. We live in a world, the Bible says, where Satan dwells (see Revelation 2:13). Going about life with a wounded soul is like living in a house in a dangerous neighborhood with a broken front door; the enemy can intrude anytime he wants to.

Just as we often struggle in vain against the effects of generational sins because we are not aware of the root of the problem, so we can feel impotent when our hearts are wounded and we do not know why. If parts of our lives are critically broken and not healed, then we feel vulnerable and lacking power in those areas—even though we are doing our best to reject Satan. Until those wounded places are made whole, we are going to lose ground.

There are many, many ways that you might have been wounded at this level. Perhaps someone spoke a word curse over you when you were young. A parent or teacher, for example, said that you were lazy or not as smart or talented or good-looking as the others. Maybe your employer cut you off professionally or a business partner took unfair advantage of you financially. Perhaps you were rejected by an ex-boyfriend, ex-girlfriend, ex-husband or ex-wife.

Most instances of trauma create clear openings for demons. Trauma shatters the soul. Children who are abused physically, verbally or sexually can be deeply broken. It is astounding how widespread the problem of sexual abuse of children is. People might not talk about it because they are ashamed, but as a pastor I have seen that it is prevalent.

Many war veterans have also experienced trauma at a deep level. Battered wives know this kind of wounding. The trauma that comes in a crisis can have the same soul-wounding effect. Sudden loneliness from losing a loved one, divorce, being in a car accident, a severe health crisis—any of these can put a person into a vulnerable place.

Even though we are on the receiving end of a wound and not at fault, nevertheless, we can fall into sin because of it. A wounded soul that is not healed is susceptible to darkness even as one with a weakened immune system is susceptible to infection.

We can come into agreement with darkness through that wound by accepting any lie that is connected to it. In other words, if we limp along believing that we can never be successful or that it was probably our fault that we were hurt as children, then we are turning from God's Word and aligning ourselves with darkness.

Suppose, for example, that an individual was verbally abused by his mother from the time he was born. He responds by walking around in shame, telling himself that her crushing words were deserved. He agrees with her put-downs and puts himself down.

Now he is contradicting God's Word. God says that He loves us, that we are valuable to Him, that we are accepted by Him, that we can do all things through Him. Rather than being in agreement with God, this man is in agreement with darkness, which is sin, and it becomes a demonic stronghold. It was the mother's sin that wounded him, but her sin has become his sin as well.

In addition, we come into agreement with darkness any time that we embrace bitterness toward the ones who hurt us. If we do not come to Jesus to heal the hurt, but rather nurse the pain, we usually build resentment and hold on to unforgiveness.

Demons that enter through an unhealed break attach themselves to the wound and feed on the inner pain. Sadly, to make things worse, the demons will work to keep the initial pain alive by promoting self-fulfilling prophecies in the person's life.

Suppose, for example, a friend of yours struggles with rejection. Maybe she was picked on as a child by the other schoolchildren. Maybe her parents made her feel like a black sheep. Maybe she was molested at a young age.

Whatever the reason, her soul was broken and a spirit of rejection moved in. Even if she has forgotten the event that caused the wound or has blocked it out of her memory, until it is brought to Jesus for healing she will struggle with a spirit of rejection.

So perhaps you are passing this friend on the street, but you are occupied with your own thoughts and do not notice her. She sees you, though, and takes it as a personal slight that you failed to make eye contact and say hello. She is certain that you are purposely rejecting her.

What does she do? She begins to distance herself from you. She acts indifferent or hurt. She might tell others that you ignored and rejected her. Then, because of her perplexing and unfair treatment, you do not enjoy being around her and actually do begin to avoid her.

> *A wounded soul can be in agreement at some level with a lie of darkness—and it is an open door to the devil.*

Thus, her agreement with darkness—the expectation of rejection—becomes self-fulfilling. This individual will probably find it difficult to give love or receive love; she expects division in relationships, and her expectation is met. The demon is camping in the open wound, keeping her pain alive.

Just recently I asked an individual how he was doing. I was sincerely interested. He answered with the words "I'm okay," but the tone and attitude were belligerent. Maybe you have talked with people like that. It seems that no matter what you say, they have such a strong spirit of rejection—which is usually rooted in fear—that they respond with suspicion and hostility. When this happens, we often take it personally and pull back, not wanting to be assaulted. Again, the fear of rejection, which is based in wounding and demonically driven, becomes a self-fulfilling prophecy.

Or suppose someone has low self-esteem because of his embarrassment from growing up in poverty. Now no matter how successful he is in life, he still has a broken place within his soul. He could have a million dollars, but demons are still going to be whispering in his ear,

You don't measure up. Other people accomplish more than you.

How do we find healing from this torment that grew out of wounding? The answer is simple but not always easy: It is to recognize the lies we are believing, replace them with the truth and forgive just as Jesus forgave. Otherwise, if we continue holding on to the torment, then we are blocking the healing balm of the Father's love.

The Lord brought this home to me some time back. He spoke to me through another dream about a house.

By the way, let me mention that as we go along I will be describing a few of the dreams that the Lord has given me. He speaks to me often in dreams; this is an important way that He communicates with His people. Acts 2:17 tells us that one of the operations of the Holy Spirit is to speak through dreams. Scripture is full of examples. One is Psalm 16:7, in which David writes that the Lord instructs his mind in the night. Perhaps you have experienced this as well.

In this dream, then, I was being chased by evil spirits. I was running all through the house trying to escape, but wherever I went, they followed me. I went into one room, and they followed me there. I ran into another room, and they followed me there. This went on for some time, and it was tormenting.

Finally, I was aware of the gaze of God. I was arrested by a beam of God's light from heaven. As I sensed His focus upon me, He caused me to see a certain person in my life I had never forgiven for a wrong done to me. He spoke to me and said, *Release that person.*

While still in the dream, I yielded and released that person, and as soon as I did, the tormentors were gone.

Are you beginning to recognize a wound in your life that has not yet been healed? Perhaps you are thinking something like this: *Yes, I know it is true. I have woundedness and unforgiveness in my soul. I know that one of the reasons I'm struggling is because I have vulnerability that came from woundedness.* For now, just make a note of that hurt.

Then be encouraged, because Jesus came to heal that wound. Look at what Scripture says. When Jesus went into the Temple to begin His ministry, He read these words from the scroll of the prophet Isaiah: "The Spirit of the Lord God is upon me, because the Lord has anointed me to bring good news to the afflicted; He has sent me to bind up the brokenhearted" (Isaiah 61:1; see Luke 4:18).

After Jesus' death and resurrection, we read that

> it was evening on that day, the first day of the week, and when the doors were shut where the disciples were, for fear of the Jews, Jesus came and stood in their midst and said to them, "Peace be with you." . . . And when He had said this, He breathed on them and said to them, "Receive the Holy Spirit. If you forgive the sins of any, their sins have been forgiven them; if you retain the sins of any, they have been retained."
>
> John 20:19, 22–23

A note in my Bible regarding verse 23 suggests that a more literal translation of the words *their sins have been forgiven them* is that these sins of others "have previously been forgiven." In other words, Jesus' death has already paid the penalty for their sins. And if we choose not to forgive, then the effect of the sin will still be alive in us. We will retain it in ourselves and will not be made whole. We will not be able to receive the fullness of the Holy Spirit that He desires for us—and, in fact, commands us to receive.

Peace is the Hebrew word *shalom*, and it is multi-dimensional. It means "complete, nothing lacking, wholeness." This is one of Yeshua's favorite words! Embracing the truth of the Word and forgiving people when they sin against us will help us receive His shalom.

Time does not heal all pain, does it? Some of us have been struggling with sins and hurts and wounds for twenty years, and they are still there. But praise Jesus! He can heal us. Time might not heal all wounds, but His shalom heals all wounds.

The Good Fight

As we close this chapter, I want you to know that you can move forward confidently to break the hold of any demons that might have entered your life through the entry points of generational patterns, personal sin and wounding by others. In the next chapter, we will learn how to eject these demons.

As you ponder the entry points that demons use, you might want to pray and ask the Father to help you see if there are any areas of access that you are not yet aware of. Here is something you might pray:

Father, I ask You to send the Holy Spirit to help me in a particular way. Give me the courage, Father, to see any areas of access in my life that have allowed demons in. Shine Your light on the particular areas where demonic activity is causing me to struggle—whether it comes from my family line, my own choice to sin, wounds I suffered or in some other way. I declare that I will not be afraid to face the truth, for You, Jesus, are truth. Thank You for helping me walk in victory. Thank You that You reign. Amen.

Jesus has given each one of us the weapons of warfare to fight the good fight of faith. We can cast down strongholds of darkness and cut to shreds the substance of the enemy in our lives. Through the Holy Spirit, you and I can walk in the light, victory and peace of Jesus, and deny demons access to our lives.

3

Three Steps to Closing the Door

Now that we understand how demons gain access to our minds and bodies, we are ready to move forward in self-deliverance. In this chapter we learn how to cancel the rights they claim and close the doors of entry.

As we begin, let's ask Jesus to cleanse our hearts and minds so that the enemy's grasp is broken. Throughout this process, our attitude should be one of encouragement. Our concerns about being set free from demons are resolved when we recognize that we are dealing with spirits, and that we can take authority over these spirits in the name of Jesus and by the power of the Holy Spirit within us. Jesus has won the victory for us, but we have to take authority over demons nonetheless.

At this point, you likely have an indication of the types of demons that possibly have access to your mind and body. The Holy Spirit might reveal more to you as we go along, so read these steps prayerfully even if you think they do not apply to you.

Step One: Confessing

I know of a man who had cheated on his wife and lived with his secret for several years. He had never told a soul. Finally, he got to the place where he could not live with his hidden brokenness any longer, and confessed to her.

When he did, something unexpected happened. His physical vision improved. He was able to see color and light that he had not been able to see all the time that he had held his dark secret. He had not realized that a film had covered him—both physically and spiritually.

Similarly, a man heard of our congregation's deliverance ministry and came for help. He said that he wanted to confess something he had never spoken of: Some years earlier, he had molested a young woman.

The simple act of acknowledging and confessing his sin made an amazing change in this man. The difference in his demeanor was physically apparent. He looked and acted like a different, more alive person.

Step one in stopping a demon's harassment is to come to Jesus and confess any sin that might have given the demon entry. Every primary access point has to do with sin. Generational sins and personal sins are obviously sin, but we have seen that being wounded can lead us into sin as well. If we believe the lie that wounded us and allow it to fester into bitterness, then we are in agreement with darkness.

As we humble our hearts before Jesus, we remember that Scripture says: "If we confess our sins, He is faithful and righteous to forgive us our sins and to cleanse us from all unrighteousness" (1 John 1:9).

Regarding the confession of family sins, in the book of Leviticus we read:

> "If they confess their iniquity and the iniquity of their forefathers, in their unfaithfulness which they committed against Me, and also in their acting with hostility against Me . . . then I will remember My covenant with Jacob, and I will remember also My covenant with Isaac, and My covenant with Abraham as well."
>
> Leviticus 26:40, 42

Please hear me. This step of confessing is not an exercise in hunting down every sin you or your family ever committed and living in fear that you might miss one. Neither is it open field day for the devil to pour condemnation on your head. The point here is to let the Holy Spirit shine His gentle light of conviction into your heart to reveal anything that you, for whatever reason, have hidden away. It is acknowledging that Jesus took every sin upon Himself at the cross, and expressing your desire to Him to make you strong in your weak areas.

Confession at the Holy Spirit's nudging can affect every aspect of your life.

If there are behaviors, attitudes or actions that you and I have chosen not to surrender to Him, or wrongful thoughts that we cannot seem to stop thinking about, or problems in our families that never seem to go away, this is the time to address them.

Let me also say that if you have never asked Jesus to be your Lord and Savior, be encouraged to do that now. He is knocking at the door of your heart, as Revelation 3:20 says. It is a simple thing to open that door. Just pray:

> *Lord Jesus, I confess that I am a sinner in need of a Savior. I believe that You died on the cross for me. I repent of my sins. Please come into my heart. I want You to be Lord and Savior of my life. Thank You, Jesus.*

Now it is time to begin confessing those sins. Look at any areas of sin in your life or your family history that the Holy Spirit is impressing on your heart. Think of anything you have a problem with or anything that runs through your family—anger, depression, alcoholism, immorality. Whatever it may be—even spirits of religion. Open your heart and mind to confessing everything that the Holy Spirit shows you.

Here is a sample prayer you might want to use. Again, remember that gentle conviction comes from the Lord; condemnation comes from the devil.

> *Thank You, Jesus, Yeshua, that You openly triumphed over every realm, entity, power and dominion of darkness. Thank You, Jesus, that You are the Head of the Church. When we cling to the shed blood of Your cross, we know that Satan has no right to our lives, no authority in our hearts, in our minds, in our emotions, in our bodies—in these earthly temples.*

Father, I ask for Your Holy Spirit to bring to my remembrance, to my heart and mind right now, any sins that You want to convict me of in my life or in my family's history. Maybe there are sins that I have never been able to face, but Your Word says that one of the operations of the Holy Spirit is to bring conviction. Open my eyes now, I pray, Lord.

I confess to You, Lord, each of the sins You have brought into my understanding.

[Confess out loud before the Lord anything that you have heard from Him. Take your time and listen for the Holy Spirit to speak anything further to your heart.]

I declare that in Yeshua the power of these sins is canceled in my life. I bind any curse from these sins from operating in my life and in the life of my family any longer.

I ask You, Lord Jesus, to release me and my family from these sins and their effects.

I thank You, Jesus, for the promise in Your Word that when we confess our sins, You are faithful and just to forgive us and cleanse us from all unrighteousness.

Thank You, Lord. Amen.

Step Two: Repenting

The next step is to repent of the sins we have just confessed. *Repent* is a word from the Bible that might seem antiquated in today's modern world. *Repent* means simply to express sorrow or regret about the wrong one has done, and to determine never to walk that way again. It means to turn from going one way and now to go in the opposite way. It is the crucial second step in closing doors that demons have been using.

I read a story recently about a man who was giving up a drug addiction. He said that he had repented, but nothing seemed to change. Then he admitted to himself the fact that he had left one marijuana cigarette in his pocket— just in case. His thinking was, *I'm going to turn away from drugs, but I might want to have just one last one.*

Your repentance is a death knell to powers of darkness.

After a while, he realized the hypocrisy of this thinking, marched himself to the trash can and threw it away.

Instantly he felt freedom. He felt something leave.

Your response after turning from sin might not be as dramatic as his, but it is as real. Confession followed by repentance delivers a deadly blow to darkness.

Here is a prayer you might want to pray:

> *King Jesus, I come to You and acknowledge that I am Yours—spirit, soul and body. In Your name, Jesus, I repent of those sins in my life that You have shown me. I also repent of those sins in my ancestors' lives that have opened the door to demons. Thank You, Jesus, for Your cleansing power. Amen.*

Step Three: Forgiving

We talked about forgiveness in the last chapter. You have probably heard powerful stories of forgiveness, and the difference it made in the lives of those who were involved—parents forgiving a drunk driver for killing their child, a woman forgiving a sexual abuser for years of childhood terror.

Most of us have probably not gone through such extreme crises, but more than likely we have forgiveness issues that we need to deal with. Maybe we are holding a grudge against a brother, a sister, a mom, a dad, someone at work, someone down the street, an aunt, an uncle. Anytime we hold on to unforgiveness, we are hindering the grace of Jesus from working freely in our lives.

On a trip to Israel not long ago, our group had a tour guide who was an Israeli woman. One of the places we visited was the Holocaust Museum, where we learned about the atrocities the Nazis had done to the Jewish people.

When we left the museum, I was struck by the response of our guide to viewing the terrible things done to her countrymen. There was great bitterness in her heart; she was visibly poisoned by it. Demonic unforgiveness was etched into her face. The Lord gave me the opportunity to talk with her about this, and I think the words I shared with her about forgiveness had an impact on her.

Unforgiveness is the poison we think we are giving someone else, but which is actually poisoning us. What people do to other people can be terrible, but if we refuse to walk in forgiveness, those hurts will cause our own souls to be demonically dark. We will be opening a door for darkness to infiltrate our own lives. The darkness will stay with us until we release and bless the one who hurt us.

If we want to get our hearts and minds clear, and close for good the doors that let demons come in and torment us, we must make a conscious decision to forgive those who have hurt us. It is vital that we let the Holy Spirit search our hearts for unforgiveness. If we are harboring animosity, bitterness or unforgiveness toward anyone, we are hindering the freedom ministry of Yeshua in our lives.

When Jesus taught us to pray the Lord's Prayer, He ended that prayer by saying, "Forgive us our sins, as we also forgive those who have sinned against us." And then He said to His disciples, "If you don't forgive other people, you are not going to experience the forgiveness of God" (see Matthew 6:12–15).

Sometimes it is easy to forgive. Other times we suffer things that we do not have the natural strength to deal with. It can be extremely hard to release forgiveness toward those who have violated us. Sometimes it is hard to forgive, release and be free of those who have hurt us. It takes the supernatural anointing of the Holy Spirit to be able to walk in this place of forgiveness, which brings wholeness.

Choosing to forgive slams shut the doors that demons like to use to invade your life.

Forgiving those who hurt you does not mean that what they did was okay. It does not mean that what they did does not hurt. It does not mean that what they did was not terribly wrong. We are not saying, "It's okay, brother. It's all right, sister. What you did wasn't really that bad."

No, that is not what we are saying at all. We are saying that we choose to obey our Master and forgive. We are saying that Jesus' death on the cross was sufficient to forgive all sin, and, based on that, we choose to extend forgiveness in His name. We choose to release and place into His hands all the bitterness we have held on to.

I think the best way to approach this is to look at Jesus. Turn your eyes away from the ones who offended you—keep those persons in the periphery—and focus your gaze on Jesus dying on the cross. As He suffered there, His eyes resting on those who spat on Him, tore out His hair, wove the crown of thorns, He said, "Father, forgive them, for they know not what they do." He forgave them. His precious blood was poured out, His life given. His death was sufficient for the sin of everybody in the world—including you and me.

Do you believe that?

Then when you are ready, ask the Holy Spirit to calm you and bring to remembrance, bring to the surface, the name of every person you need to forgive and release. If this is painful for you, do this step with a pastor, counselor or mature prayer partner.

Then, realizing that Jesus has forgiven you, be willing to look at Jesus forgiving each one.

Keep your eyes on Jesus, not on the people who wounded you. If you look at the people who wounded you, all you are going to feel is shame, anger, vengeance, hurt or bitterness. Remember Peter. He was able to walk on water as long as he kept his eyes on Jesus. But as soon as he looked around at the wild waves and felt the great gusts of wind, he was overwhelmed and sank.

It can be the same way with forgiveness.

Some of us have been so wounded that when we look at the person or the situation that hurt us we get overwhelmed. We get sucked down again into the emotions we have carried in our hearts.

Keep your gaze off the people and on Jesus. Meditate on Him. See His arms open wide. Feel love emanating from Him as He says, "Father, forgive them for they know not what they do."

Now, with your eyes on Jesus, simply say, *"I forgive them. I release them."*

Every time you are tempted to fall into feelings of shame or unforgiveness, turn your eyes back to Jesus and say, "Jesus, I release them just as You did. Amen."

Crossing the River

Let me give you an illustration here that might help. Imagine that there is a red river of Jesus' blood flowing past your feet. Here you are on one side with all of the issues of the generations, and all of your own sins, and all of your negative responses to the sins that were committed against you.

You have confessed all of the sins that the Holy Spirit has brought to your remembrance. You have repented of them. Now you can make the choice to cross that river of forgiveness by faith.

Here are some words to help you as you walk through this vital step of self-deliverance:

In Your name, Jesus, I ask Your forgiveness for the sins in my ancestry and in my own life.

I forgive myself for my wrong decisions and actions.

I forgive everyone who has committed any sin against me.

[You might want to name them if this will help you feel greater release from them.]

I ask You, Father God, to release me right now from any operation that is happening in my life from the realm of darkness. Release me from any demonic activity that is touching me, influencing me or holding a place within me because of the sins of my past generations, my own bad choices and my wrong responses to the wounds I have received from others.

Lord Jesus, I ask You to pour out Your grace and cover over all of this by Your blood.

Now I close every door of entry. I declare that Satan and demonic activity can no longer enter my life through those doors. I bind any future demonic activity from coming through those places.

Thank You, Jesus. Help me to keep my eyes on You. Amen.

Now imagine yourself crossing through Jesus' blood over to the other side. Can you imagine that? Believe that unforgiveness has been washed away by the river.

Then believe that your generational sins have been washed in the river. Believe that your own sins have been washed in the river. Believe that your agreement with lies that came through wounding has been washed in the river.

One more thing here. Sometimes we hurt other people and need to ask them to forgive us. If there is someone you have wounded and whose forgiveness you need to ask, take this to the Lord in prayer to see if it is a situation that you need to go and ask forgiveness for.

Pressing On

With these prayers to Jesus, you have powerfully struck the darkness that has been dominating your life.

If the enemy tries to taunt you into believing that your efforts have been futile, simply turn to Jesus with words of praise for His wonderful and transforming work in your life.

This is just the beginning, but it is a new beginning to the journey of a lifetime. We learn to walk in freedom as we press on.

In the next three chapters, we are going to look at two aspects of our position in Jesus that prepare us for casting the demons out. These are "truth encounters" and "power encounters."

Put briefly, we know that the truth will make us free. That is what I mean by truth encounters. Truth combats and defeats the lies of the enemy that put us into captivity.

But first we need to understand why we can speak truth so effectively. It is because of power encounters—our authority and our power in Jesus. In other words, truth sets us free *when* we speak it with the appropriate power and authority.

And, as we will see next, our position of strength comes out of a sense of weakness that will cause us to rely on Jesus. Like Paul, we say, "When I am weak, then I am strong" (2 Corinthians 12:10).

4

Stand in Authority, Move in Power

I remember the first time I was involved in a deliverance ministry back in the 1980s. I went with an experienced pastor to the home of a man who had asked for help. This guy was obviously demon-inhabited. He was infested.

It was my first time, and I was a little nervous. So, what did I do? I began to scream at the demons as loudly as I could. It was the only thing I knew to do. I thought something like, *If I scream loud enough, maybe they will listen to me. If I scream louder, maybe I'll have authority.*

Afterward the pastor took me aside and said, "You know, when your blade's sharp, you don't have to cut so hard."

I had no idea of the position that I had in Jesus to drive out demons. The concept of the power encounter—which is a mixture of both the authority and power of Jesus—was an important lesson for me.

Until you and I understand our positioning as believers, we can go through all the mechanics of deliverance, and the results will be negligible. We will have little effect because we are not using the resources available to us.

Power and authority work in tandem, but they are quite different. Authority is given to us. The power to use that authority needs to be developed.

What Authority Do We Have?

After His death and resurrection, Jesus appeared to His disciples and made this declaration: "All authority has been given to Me in heaven and on earth" (Matthew 28:18).

In other words, the deal is done. King Jesus conquered death, conquered every power of darkness, conquered every demon from hell, rose from the grave, ascended to the right hand of God and reigns over all. The Father has "put all things in subjection under [Jesus'] feet" (Ephesians 1:22).

Furthermore, the Bible tells us that the Father also "gave Him as head over all things to the church, which is His body, the fullness of Him who fills all in all" (Ephesians 1:22–23).

Jesus has been given to the Church as her Head. Our future is now secure in Him. Romans 8:38–39 assures us that neither death nor life, neither things present nor things to come can separate us from the love of God.

So, to recap, Jesus has all authority, He reigns over all, and He heads the Church. But there is more.

We read in another portion of Scripture about the mystery of the Gospel. This is the mystery, Paul said: "Christ in you" (see Colossians 1:27).

Jesus Himself—the One who according to Ephesians 1:20–21 was raised from the dead and is seated at the right hand of the Father "in the heavenly places, far above all rule and authority and power and dominion, and every name that is named, not only in this age but also in the one to come"—that very Jesus *lives inside of you and me.*

And He has given His Church full permission to operate in His name: "Behold, I have given you authority . . . over all the power of the enemy" (Luke 10:19). This includes casting out demons. When we take our stand in Christ, we operate in His authority by the power of the Holy Spirit. We can drive out

> *Jesus expects you to use His full authority to counter evil.*

demons and every form of darkness from our lives. We have authority in Jesus to speak to these spirits, and they *must* obey.

Authority basically means the right to act. We never have to pray to receive authority. We can pray, however, that we will understand the authority that we have in Jesus.

God's Power Supply

Many years ago, shortly after I had finished Bible school, I had an experience that I have never forgotten because it was so impressive.

In the middle of the night, I awoke to see a vision before my eyes. It was a dark night on the ocean. As I looked at the vision I saw a huge, beautiful warship cutting through the deep waters. Then I felt as though I was standing on the bow of the ship, looking out over the vastness of the sea. At the same time, I could feel the power, the beauty and the majesty of the great vessel. It was thrilling.

The vision had come out of nowhere; I was not thinking about warships. It made a significant impact because it was from another realm. For a long time I did not understand why God had given it to me or what it meant.

Over the years the Lord revealed to me that this warship was a picture of each of His children. I believe that when you and I exercise the authority that God has given us through the Spirit of God, who is a possession of every believer, the darkness can no longer have dominion over us. We can stand securely in Jesus' authority and conquer the darkness—even as I stood high on the bow of the great warship as it charged over the dark ocean.

Our authority in Jesus is a wonderful gift from God, but we need something additional to be effective in the spiritual battle: We need His power. Using our warship image, it is His power—His strength and might—that causes the ship to glide along smoothly. Even with His authority, we cannot operate effectively in the spiritual battle without that power.

We do not have this strength in ourselves. The apostle Paul makes it clear that Jesus' power is made most evident through our frailty:

> And [Jesus] has said to me, "My grace is sufficient for you, for power is perfected in weakness." . . . Therefore I am well content with weaknesses, with insults, with distresses,

with persecutions, with difficulties, for Christ's sake; for when I am weak, then I am strong.

2 Corinthians 12:9–10

Paul was going through a time of weakness and testing and pain, but he acknowledged a purpose in it. In that place of hardship, he knew that he could not help himself. He had only one place to go, and that was to God. He was being made strong and learning that God was faithful and trustworthy.

Anytime you discern your dependence on God, you are standing in a powerful place of warfare.

Jesus modeled this very thing for us when He entered the wilderness after His baptism. He ate nothing during those forty days. Why do you think He did that? I believe one of the reasons is that fasting, which is what He did, is a voluntary form of putting oneself in weakness. He was turning to God in weakness so that He could be filled with strength. After those forty days, He came out and returned to Galilee "in the power of the Spirit" (Luke 4:14).

You and I need to follow His example if we are going to move effectively against darkness. God makes us strong against the enemy when we come to Him hungering for Him. He cannot fill what is already full. If we are full of ourselves, full of our pride and other things, the Lord has no space to occupy. We cannot be full of the world and expect to be given His strength. But when we are hungry and desperate and cry out in our weakness, then we get filled.

That is also why Jesus began the Beatitudes with these words: "Blessed are the poor in spirit, for theirs is the kingdom of heaven" (Matthew 5:3). There is no shortcut to this. When we are poor in spirit, weak in the natural and clinging to God, then He brings forth His strength in our lives. We are acknowledging that we derive our substance from Him. We are looking to Him as our source.

If you are in a desperate place, you are in a good position to see your dependence on God and to let Him make you strong in the Spirit.

The Reality of His Presence

Getting free starts with power encounters. God gives us His authority, and He works His power in us as we come to Him in our weakness. In the meantime, we grow stronger in the power He is developing in us.

A friend of mine, whom I will call Jarrod, was attending a worship service not long ago, but was finding it hard to focus on the Lord. The problem was a group of rowdy teens sitting behind him. They were not bad kids, but they were singing loudly, laughing and, in general, seeming to enjoy being disruptive. Some of the people near Jarrod turned to give them disapproving looks.

Jarrod put up with it for a few minutes. But then he had had enough. Without turning around or speaking out loud, Jarrod took authority over the spirits that were egging on the teens' behavior. He commanded them to be quiet.

In that moment, shalom came over the teens. The chaotic behavior ceased. They were calm and quiet.

Jarrod's authority in Yeshua gave him the right to deal with those demons, but it was power that drove them out. Power is influence. It is a demonstrable, substantial force. The power that we have through the Holy Spirit allows us to use Jesus' name in such a way that demons tremble.

Think of the position of police officers. An officer has authority as shown by the badge he or she wears. Some people, however, have no respect for authority. In dealing with them, an officer has to use power. He or she has to get out the billy club or the Taser or the gun. Just the same, demons respond to authority, but sometimes they are belligerent and need to be confronted with power.

In the case with Jarrod, they obeyed him the first time he commanded them. But it can happen that believers— even those who have significant ministries in the realm of deliverance—will have to keep on commanding a demon to leave before it will obey.

Sometimes this happens because we need to grow in the use of power, and sometimes the demons are just particularly stubborn. They might laugh or declare that they do not have to listen, they do not have to leave, et cetera, et cetera. But when you and I persist because we understand our authority in Jesus' name and our right to use His power, then eventually the demons will break and leave.

Relationship Is Key

Understanding our authority and power is something that we grow into more and more. We develop in power predominantly as we disengage from the world. This helps us become more in touch with the Spirit of God, and get more discernment about what is happening in the spiritual realm around us. The thing that truly satisfies is not the connection we have to the world, or even to people, but to the Lord and to the reality of His presence. It is relationship with Him that makes the difference in whether or not we gain victory over the powers of darkness.

Any attempt at deliverance apart from relationship with Jesus is bound to fail.

Many people have true saving faith in God, but they relate to Him primarily as if He is only in heaven. They fail to realize that Jesus is within them. In other words, many people's concept of God is that He exists somewhere out there. But we remember Jesus' words in Revelation 3:20: "Behold, I stand at the door and knock. If anyone hears my voice and opens the door, I will come in to him and eat with him, and he with me" (Revelation 3:20).

The place that satisfies is when we know Him in us, and fellowship with Him from within. This experience of knowing Him from the inside brings peace, satisfaction and revelation of our authority and power in Him.

A story told in Acts 19 illustrates the vital place of relationship with Jesus in our spiritual battle with darkness. In Paul's day, Jewish exorcists could be hired professionally. This story describes some of these exorcists who watched Paul do great works in the name of Jesus. They knew of Jesus by reputation, but had no personal relationship with Him.

God was performing extraordinary miracles by the hands of Paul, so that . . . the evil spirits went out. But also some of the Jewish exorcists, who went from place to place, attempted to name over those who had the evil spirits the name of the Lord Jesus, saying, "I adjure you by Jesus whom Paul preaches."

Acts 19:11–13

The sons of a chief priest named Sceva were among these professional exorcists. Because they were not believers in Jesus, they had no connection to His authority and power.

Seven sons of one Sceva, a Jewish chief priest, were doing this. And the evil spirit answered and said to them, "I recognize Jesus, and I know about Paul, but who are you?"

And the man, in whom was the evil spirit, leaped on them and subdued all of them and overpowered them, so they fled out of the house naked and wounded.

verses 14–16

The individual whom the seven men were trying to cast the demon out of turned on them, beat them up and sent them flying.

Do you see that there has to be a relationship with Jesus for His power to be developed in our lives? (We will talk more about this relationship in chapter 7.) People cannot use Jesus' name flippantly and expect demons to honor their position.

Rather, Yeshua said that the one who abides in Him will bear much fruit (see John 15:5). If you are connected to Jesus, if you have received Him as your Savior and asked Him to be Lord over your life, then I want you to know that you already have authority and you can grow in power. Jesus said, "He who overcomes will inherit these things"

(Revelation 21:7). You might have to stick with it, but I promise you: You *will* win. This is not optional. Demons will obey you.

Becoming Enlightened

God wants us to understand who Jesus is and who we are in Him. Look at these words that Paul wrote to the Ephesian church:

> [I pray that] the God of our Lord Jesus Christ . . . may give to you a spirit of wisdom and of revelation in the knowledge of Him. I pray the eyes of your heart may be enlightened, so that you will know . . . what are the riches of the glory of His inheritance in the saints, and what is the surpassing greatness of His power toward us who be-lieve. These [realities] are in accordance with the working of the strength of his might which He brought about in Christ, when He raised Him from the dead . . . and He put all things in subjection under His feet.
>
> Ephesians 1:17–20, 22

God wants the eyes of our hearts to be enlightened. He wants us to understand "the surpassing greatness of His power toward us who believe." This is our inheritance— "the riches of the glory of His inheritance in the saints." As we keep this process of self-deliverance before God in prayer, He will help us understand the authority we have, and will help us develop and walk in the power He has given us.

Satan wants us to feel impotent. He wants to make us feel as though we have no authority, no power—and that he does not have to listen to us. He is hoping to keep us from our inheritance. But the power we have within us is the same power that raised Jesus from the dead and seated Him at the right hand of God. It is the power that broke every demon in hell.

Satan wants you to feel impotent. God wants you to feel His power.

This is why Paul directed us to pray that the eyes of our hearts will be enlightened: so that we can know the power at work within us. This power is in accordance with the strength of the might of God Himself. Furthermore, Paul prayed and asked Father God to develop this power in us.

Ephesians 3:14–16 is one of my favorite portions in the entire Word of God:

> For this reason I bow my knees before the Father, from whom every family in heaven and on earth derives its name, that He would grant you, according to the riches of His glory, to be strengthened with power through His Spirit in the inner man.

We should likewise be praying that God will strengthen us in our inner man. As we step into faith and break the evil binding us, we grow more and more into the realization that we do have power, and that God is strengthening us with power in our inner man. At first we might have a tendency not to believe this because it is going to seem as though nothing is happening. We wonder, *Did it work? Did the demons obey me? Did they listen to me? Has anything really changed?*

I want to encourage you: If you make a commitment to believe that you do have authority, that you do have power, then you are going to find over time that unclean spirits are subject to you. You must refuse to be intimidated or conquered. You just keep commanding in the name of Jesus the Messiah (or Jesus the Son of God or Jesus of Nazareth—there is no one way this has to be worded). All authority in heaven and on earth belongs to Jesus. You have His full authority to cast out demons. You can keep commanding by the power of God's Spirit.

When you keep standing, you are going to be filled with joy as you begin to experience the results. When you know, and the demons know that you know, they are going to leave.

I hope that this gives you better understanding and vision about who you and I really are. We should walk not with our eyes downcast in defeat but with our heads up because this is our inheritance as the saints.

Continuing in Power

Earlier we noted Jesus' teaching about continuing in His Word. He said: "If you continue in My word, then you are truly disciples of Mine; and you will know the truth, and the truth will make you free" (John 8:31–32). This process of entering into freedom is continuous. In other words, we need to be *continuing* in His Word, *continuing* in grace, *continuing* to be strengthened, *continuing* to discern the darkness, *continuing* to be enlightened about the authority and the power that we have. And as we do, we become more and more free.

Psalm 18 gives us a good picture of this ongoing authority/power advancement. David began by crying out to God: "In my distress I called upon the LORD, and cried to my God for help; He heard my voice out of His temple, and my cry for help before Him came into His ears" (verse 6).

David was desperate for God. He knew that he had no life without God. Then, as the words of the psalm proceed, we see David moving into offensive action against darkness. He said this:

> For by You I can run upon a troop; and by my God I can leap over a wall. . . . For who is God, but the LORD? And who is a rock, except our God, the God who girds me with strength and makes my way blameless? He makes my feet like hinds' feet, and sets me upon my high places. He trains my hands for battle, so that my arms can bend a bow of bronze. . . . I pursued my enemies and overtook them, and I did not turn back until they were consumed. I shattered them, so they were not able to rise; they fell under my feet. For You have girded me with strength for battle; You have subdued under me those who rose up against me. You have also made my enemies turn their backs to me; and I destroyed those who hated me.
>
> Psalm 18:29, 31–34, 37–40

Did demons hate David? Yes. Do demons hate you and me? Yes. And they are not going to go away unless we make them go away. David continued:

> Then I beat them fine as the dust before the wind; I emptied them out as the mire of the streets. You have delivered me from the contentions of the people; You have placed me as head of the nations; a people whom I have not known

71

serve me. As soon as they hear, they obey me; foreigners submit to me. Foreigners fade away, and come trembling out of their fortresses. The LORD lives, and blessed be my rock; and exalted be the God of my salvation, the God who executes vengeance for me, and subdues peoples under me. He delivers me from my enemies; surely You lift me above those who rise up against me; You rescue me from the violent man.

Psalm 18:42–48

David began his battle by crying out to God in his weakness: "In my distress I called upon the LORD, and cried to my God for help." From there he moved into an offensive posture: "I pursued my enemies and overtook them." And from there he moved on to utterly destroy his adversaries: "I did not turn back until they were consumed. I shattered them, so that they were not able to rise; they fell under my feet."

This is the way our fight against darkness proceeds: from crying out to God in our weakness, to rising up in strength on the offense, to becoming so confident and courageous that we utterly destroy our enemies.

Pray and Fight

As you begin to practice what you are learning, you are going to realize that you have authority, and then you are going to come against the enemy with power. This combination defines the power encounter of self-deliverance. In the next chapter we will begin speaking to the demons, enacting the truth encounter. Demons are defeated when we recognize and reject their lies.

We have been called to reign in the heavens with Christ Jesus, to live in love and joy and peace. This is the heritage of the servants of the Lord. This is the destiny and the call on each one of our lives, and if we believe it and contend for it, we will enter into it.

Keep standing in the fight. When you grasp your power and authority in Jesus, demons will obey you.

Later, in chapter 8, we are going to talk extensively about our place of aggression in the matter of self-deliverance. We pray and we fight. Jesus' power is perfected in our weakness, and we are enabled to move forward boldly like a great warship cruising along, powerful and steady over the ocean at midnight.

Jesus, I pray that You will help me understand the authority that You have given me in the spiritual realm. I pray, like the apostle Paul, that You will enlighten my eyes to understand the hope of my calling, the riches of Your glory that dwell within me and the surpassing greatness of Your power toward me.

King David wrote in his psalm that You trained him for battle. Jesus, please train me in this spiritual battle to defeat those spirits that have been tormenting me.

I ask You to forgive me for being connected to the outer world in a way that blinds me to You and to Your truth. Your Word says that in Your light, we see light.

I know that Your Church has been called to victory over every spirit coming against us because we have been raised with You, and seated with You in heavenly places. The Kingdom of God is life and joy and freedom and hope in the Holy Spirit. Strengthen me to live in that realm now.

Jesus, I believe and declare that because of You, I no longer have to live under torment. I can enter into a realm of freedom in You, because You said that whoever the Son sets free is free indeed! Thank You, Jesus. Amen.

5

Should We Speak to Demons?

Many of us take seriously the privilege of communicating with our heavenly Father. We understand and rejoice that we can talk *with* God. But did you realize that we must also talk *at* evil spirits?

Too often we fall short when it comes to commanding the devil and his demons. Some people, I think, shy away from direct contact with evil spirits because they fear stirring them up and being overtaken. Others consider it presumption to address the devil directly: *Jesus could, of course, but who am I to do that?* Others think it is futile, so why try? Bottom line, it feels safer just to let sleeping dogs lie.

The misunderstanding of our position in Jesus, alongside lack of knowledge about dealing with evil spirits, has kept countless believers in bondage. But we have learned that when we do nothing, the devil wins.

The alternative for followers of Yeshua is to embrace the power and authority that we have in Him—the power encounter—and then move forward with confidence into the truth encounter. This next aspect of self-deliverance is a simple matter of *knowing* why and how we address the evil spirits that are tormenting us, *commanding* them to leave, and then *maintaining* awareness of our thoughts.

In this chapter we will explore the principles of why we speak at demons and learn the few simple commands that remove them from our lives. In the next chapter, we will learn how to judge our thoughts and reject any that are coming from evil spirits, so that the demons we evict cannot return.

Why Do We Address Demons?

The Bible makes clear to us why we speak to demonic spirits: If we never learn to do so, we will never move forward into freedom from darkness. Think again of the violent demoniac in the country of the Gadarenes. The people in that area had tried every means they knew of to subdue him, even simply to clothe him, but he remained unchanged: "Constantly, night and day, he was screaming among the tombs and in the mountains, and gashing himself with stones" (Mark 5:5; see verses 1–15).

Speaking at demons is not the same as having a conversation with them.

Until Jesus came and spoke to the demons commanding them to leave, the man had no hope of freedom.

76

Scripture gives us many examples of winning the battle against evil spirits by speaking at them. (I sometimes use the phrase *speak at demons* rather than *speak to demons*, which could imply conversation.) Look again, for instance, at the story of the temptation of Jesus in the wilderness.

> Jesus was led up by the Spirit into the wilderness to be tempted by the devil. And after He had fasted forty days and forty nights, He then became hungry. And the tempter came and said to Him, "If You are the Son of God, command that these stones become bread."
>
> But [Jesus] answered and said, "It is written, 'Man shall not live on bread alone, but on every word that proceeds out of the mouth of God.'"
>
> Matthew 4:1–4

The text goes on to tell us (see verses 5–11) that the devil then tempted Jesus to prove that He was the Son of God by throwing Himself from the pinnacle of the Temple. Jesus responded by quoting from the Torah: "It is written, 'You shall not put the Lord your God to the test.'"

Lastly, the devil offered Jesus all the kingdoms of the world if He would only fall down and worship him. Notice Jesus' words: "Go, Satan! For it is written, 'You shall worship the Lord your God, and serve Him only.'"

What happened next? "The devil left Him."

Jesus was not having a dialogue with Satan in the sense of conversing with him to get his opinion. Jesus was fully engaged in battle with Satan, and He won by speaking Scripture. He was, in effect, telling Satan to shut up, to get behind Him, to be gone. Jesus was cutting the devil's legs off, and He did this by speaking at him.

In Matthew 16:21–23 we see another example. Jesus was telling His disciples that

> He must go to Jerusalem, and suffer many things from the elders and chief priests and scribes, and be killed, and be raised up on the third day. Peter took Him aside and began to rebuke Him, saying, "God forbid it, Lord! This shall never happen to You." But [Jesus] turned and said to Peter, "Get behind Me, Satan! You are a stumbling block to Me; for you are not setting your mind on God's interests, but man's.'"

Jesus was not talking metaphorically to Peter here. He was giving a literal command to the devil.

Jesus also taught His followers to set people free by speaking directly to demons. The seventy disciples that He sent out in ministry returned to Him rejoicing that demons were subject to them when they gave commands in His name.

Acts 16 tells the story of the slave girl who chased after Paul and Silas while they were traveling through Thyatira. This girl was possessed by a spirit of divination by which she could tell fortunes. She followed them for many days, crying out continually that Paul and Silas were servants of God.

Finally, Paul became so annoyed at this he turned toward her and said, "'I command you in the name of Jesus Christ to come out of her!' And [the evil spirit] came out at that very moment" (Acts 16:18).

We learn from Scripture, then, that we do not just speak to God; we also speak into the spiritual atmosphere of darkness, commanding spirits of darkness to go. Otherwise, if we let the enemy continue to move through our brains and bring anxiety and fear and all other types of defilement, and we fail to do anything about it, we will be plagued by that distress our whole lives. Until we begin to stand up in the righteousness of Jesus and command these spirits to go, they will not go.

Obedience to the Spoken Word

There are appropriate times, then, for believers to address evil spirits and take authority over them. Jesus "cast out the spirits with a word" (Matthew 8:16). He dislodged and detached demons, and He did it by speaking to them. He spoke to the presence and power of darkness, and it obeyed.

By nature, God is a speaking God. When He created the heavens and the earth, He *spoke*. He *said*, "Let there be light."

What begins in the heart must come out of the mouth for the action to be completed. This is where our faith as believers is released. Look at this verse that demonstrates this principle:

> If you confess with your mouth Jesus as Lord, and believe in your heart that God raised Him from the dead, you will be saved; for with the heart a person believes, resulting in righteousness, *and with the mouth he confesses, resulting in salvation.*
>
> Romans 10:9–10, emphasis added

This shows the marriage between believing in the heart and speaking with the mouth to accomplish the purposes of God. You see, when we speak, the inner life is released. The manifestation of salvation takes place. It is only after what is in the heart is confessed in words, whether through our inner man or out loud with our physical mouths, that the transaction is completed in the spirit realm.

This is why the Holy Spirit came at Pentecost as a fiery tongue, a speaking oracle—because the nature of our relationship with God is communication, and communication takes place through words.

Now, as we grow in this and start to put into practice the concept of speaking to evil spirits for the purpose of self-deliverance, we also begin to recognize that we do indeed have authority. We become more and more aware of what is going on. We begin to speak with power more confidently. We get sharper and come out of darkness and into the light.

This is not going to happen overnight. But as you start speaking to these encroaching spirits, you will begin to see things change. You will see that the place is closing through which the enemy once had free access to you. As your strength grows, you will know for certain that you have the ability to defend yourself. And more than this, you will take territory in and for God in the realm of the Spirit.

There is no doubt that self-deliverance works. The only question is, Will we do it? Jesus said, "If anyone is willing to do [the Father's] will, he will know of the teaching, whether it is of God or whether I speak from Myself" (John 7:17).

I tell you right now: If you do this for a period of time, you will discover that it works.

Should Demons Be Allowed to Speak?

Unless Jesus was asking demons a specific question, He did not permit them to speak. Here is an example.

> When evening came, after the sun had set, they began bringing to Him . . . those who were demon-possessed. And the whole city had gathered at the door. And He . . . cast out many demons; and *He was not permitting the demons to speak*, because they knew who He was.
>
> Mark 1:32–34, emphasis added

Letting demons talk would be the same as acknowledging them and giving them position. The only way to deal with evil spirits is to recognize that they are absolutely foul and defiled; they deserve no attention at all. They do not deserve to have a voice. They do not deserve to have a right to explain themselves. We reject them completely and command them to get out.

The way Jesus dealt with the demons in the man from the country of the Gadarenes might seem at first like a contradiction of what I am telling you.

When the demoniac, the man who could not be bound even by strong chains, saw Jesus, he

> ran up and bowed down before Him; and shouting with a loud voice, he said, "What business do we have with each other, Jesus, Son of the Most High God? I implore You by God, do not torment me!" for He had been saying to him, "Come out of the man, you unclean spirit!"
>
> Mark 5:6–8

Then Jesus seemed to change His approach. Rather than continuing to command the demon out, He asked a question: "What is your name?"

The demon replied, "My name is Legion; for we are many."

In this instance, Jesus was directing the demon to name himself in order to expose the entity. Once the spirits were exposed, He drove them all out. Fully aware of Jesus' authority over them, the defeated demons begged to be allowed to inhabit a herd of about two thousand swine, which Jesus permitted.

At the end of the story, the people of the region came to see what was going on, and they found the former demoniac "sitting down, clothed and in his right mind" (Mark 5:15).

Casting Evil Spirits Out

Before we begin with actual commands of self-deliverance, let me mention that, personally, I do not think it is necessary to say the words *in Jesus' name* every time I speak a command to evil spirits. As far as I am concerned, self-deliverance is always in Jesus' name. I am purchased by the blood of the Lamb, and Jesus Himself is in me. Jesus said to His followers, "I have given *you* authority over all the power of the enemy." So when I give a command, it *is* in Jesus' name by the power of the Holy Spirit because I am in Jesus and Jesus is in me.

Even so, usually I will say *in Jesus' name*. The point is that you and I understand *our* authority in Jesus over the devil.

Okay, let's get started. Here are four steps of self-deliverance that will help you cast out the evil spirits that are infesting your life.

Step One: Identify the Presence of a Demon

When you want to command an evil spirit to leave, it can be helpful to identify the spirit that is tormenting you. We have looked at this in several ways, and you probably have a good idea of which demons you are dealing with. If not, you have the option to take the time to think further. Ask yourself:

How are evil spirits operating in my life?
What wounds might they have attached to?
What lies are they speaking to me?
What functions do they fill?
In what way is my life hindered or crippled?
What do I think I need in order to be happy?
What am I addicted to?
Is Satan fortifying that addiction?
Am I willing to give it up?

If you have ever heard a little voice in your head that says *I cannot be fulfilled unless I* (fill in the blank) or *I am worthless because I* (fill in the blank) or *God is never going to hear my prayers because I* (fill in the blank), then you can get a sense of which demon is walking around with you and feeding you lies, keeping you unhappy and dissatisfied.

If you are still not sure of the demon's identity, you can try commanding the demon to tell you his name.

A man in our congregation came to me after one of our services and said that he had commanded the evil spirit that was tormenting him to reveal himself. He had said these words: "Evil spirit, in the name of the Lord Jesus Christ I command you to reveal yourself to me. Who are you and what is your name?"

All of a sudden, a name popped into his head. It was a literal name: "Sexton." With that information, he dispatched the demon easily.

Here is a prayer you might want to pray. This prayer will help you ask the Holy Spirit to put His finger on any demons that are troubling you and force them to identify themselves. This can be helpful in understanding which demonic stronghold you are dealing with.

Jesus, thank You that You gave Your Church authority over demons and over all the powers of darkness. I choose to exercise that authority now.

Holy Spirit, I ask You to put Your light and pressure on any demonic squatter in me, causing him to surface. Cause his function to be made known.

You can also speak to the demon at this point, if you want to do so:

"I command you, demon, to reveal who you are, what you represent, what your function has been, what your name is. I command you to be exposed right now, by the authority of Yahweh God and of King Jesus. I command you to be exposed by the light of King Jesus and the glory of God."

Has something presented itself to your mind? Do you have a sense, an "inner knowing" of the demons that are troubling you? Maybe a name you have not heard before, a picture, a picture of a word, a function—lying, greed, self-pity, sickness?

Does it seem like a demon of hostility, a demon of rage, a demon of jealousy? Is it a controlling spirit, a perfectionist spirit, a spirit of infirmity? Is it a manipulative spirit? Is it a Jezebel spirit trying to control other people through you? It could be anything. I have even heard of a demon of mischief.

Any spirit that counters Scripture is automatically demonic. Suppose you struggle with a spirit whose function is to make you feel inept when it comes to spiritual matters. The Bible says that you have the mind of Christ, so you know that the voice speaking self-recrimination belongs to a demon.

While it can be helpful when speaking to a demon to know the particular name, we do not have to have it in order to cast the demon out. It is the same with the demon's function. That can be helpful but is not vital.

If you can name that ball of demonic energy that you are up against, then you can move forward with confidence. But if you cannot name it, you can move forward just as confidently. In the story of the demon known as Legion, Jesus did not proceed to identify each and every one of the great number of demons tormenting the man.

Personally, I have never asked a demon a question regarding his name or function while pursuing deliverance for myself. For me, the identity of a defiled spirit comes by way of discernment. I will sometimes ask demons to give their names while in ministry to help other people get free. In these instances I might say something like: "In the name of Jesus of Nazareth, I call you before the throne of Yahweh God and command you to reveal your name."

We need to understand, though, that if we ask evil spirits a question, there is no guarantee they will respond with the truth. They could just as well be lying.

I think the solution for us is to realize that we should not get hung up on trying to get a name; sometimes we do not even need to narrow down the particular function. If all you have to go on is the sense that you are dealing with something that is demonic, then you are in effect naming it. You are sensing that you are dealing with a spirit from the realm of darkness that is separate from yourself. If nothing else, you can use the words *you defiled spirit*.

Whether or not you know the identity or function of the demon, you can proceed to the next step. If you know only that you are dealing with a defiled spirit, you can command it to leave.

Step Two: Command the Spirit to Go

Just as Jesus cast out demons with a word, so you can command evil spirits to leave. You might say something like: "I reject you, defiled spirit, and I command you to leave me in the name of Jesus."

You can do this out loud or you can speak through your heart and mind, however the Lord directs you. Sometimes I speak out loud; sometimes I speak at demons through my inner man, especially if in a public place.

Regarding speaking to demons quietly in our own hearts and minds, I believe that demons can hear our inner thoughts. This is nothing to be afraid of. In fact, it can be helpful. Suppose you are at your job as a dental hygienist or bank teller and need to address demons that are trying to slip into your mind. You do not want to make public the fact that you are commanding evil spirits to leave you alone. You can take care of this quietly and confidently. Remember, we are dealing not with the physical world, but with the realm of the spirit.

After this step, you might not feel as though much has happened. That is what Satan wants you to believe. Be assured: Change is happening. Change comes little by little, but you will get victory and enter into freedom. Keep pressing on. Make up your mind not to give up. Jesus has overcome and He lives in you now. The victory is already won. You just need to press through to enter into it.

Step Three: Confess the Positive

Now it is time to speak the opposite of the lies that the demons have been telling you. The most powerful way to speak the positive is to counter the enemy's lies with the truth of Scripture. Continue to replace each demonic thought with a "God thought."

Suppose that a demon's job has been to fill you with thoughts of hatred toward somebody. You became aware that demons were filling your head with thoughts of judgment, condemnation and accusation toward that person. You commanded the defiled spirits to leave, and they had to leave. But now you need to fill the space left vacant.

You might say something like this:

Father God, You tell us in Your Word to love one another. I know that You love this person. I choose to agree with You. I bless this person. I bless you [name of person]. I bless you in the name of the Lord.

Suppose demons were making you afraid that if you went after them they would really hurt you. In this case you could replace that lie by speaking the promise of Scripture that nothing shall by any means hurt you. Thank God that He loves you and that you are protected in Him.

If a demon has been tormenting you with overwhelming shame for who you are, speak the truth that there is no condemnation for those who are in Christ Jesus. He loves you. You are valuable to Him. You are accepted by Him. You can do all things through Him.

You get the idea. This is a very important part of self-deliverance. We need to fill our hearts and minds with the positive in the areas that have been polluted. We need to strengthen those weak and vulnerable spots with the truth of Scripture. We must take the initiative and leave demons no space to refill.

Step Four: Be Aware That Demons Will Try to Return

As you put into practice the principles of self-deliverance that we are exploring, you are engaging in spiritual warfare. At this point, you have learned how to drive demons out of your mind and body.

This is victory!

It might not seem at first as though much has changed. As I have mentioned, this is normal. You might be having many of the same negative thoughts you had before starting this process of self-deliverance. There is a big difference, though. As the demons are loosening their grip on you, being dislodged from you and being forced to let go, their attack comes at you from the outside rather than from than the inside.

As we learned at the beginning of this book, demonic spirits are constantly seeking to assault us: "For our struggle is not against flesh and blood, but against the rulers, against the powers, against the world forces of this darkness, against the spiritual forces of wickedness in the heavenly places" (Ephesians 6:12).

Remember the words of Luke 4:13: After Jesus had defeated Satan in the wilderness, the devil "left Him until an opportune time."

You are gaining victory over the powers of darkness. At the same time, the enemy opposes your new walk into freedom. The more you keep on walking in the light, the more you will immobilize evil spirits and the more victory you will gain.

This growing into victory involves discernment, which we are developing in this process. The Bible says that "the mature . . . because of practice have their senses trained to discern good and evil" (Hebrews 5:14). We understand, grow in and prove the will of the Lord by practicing it.

As we grow in discernment we become keener at perceiving where the thoughts that are entering our minds are coming from. In the chapter that follows, we learn more about our thinking process, and the simple command that keeps the devil from reentering our hearts and minds.

6

Keeping Control of Your Thoughts

Demons have a desire for us. We see this spelled out in the words God spoke to an angry young man named Cain: "Sin is crouching at the door," the Lord said to him, "*and its desire is for you*, but you must master it" (Genesis 4:7, emphasis added).

Demons have a desire to steal, kill and destroy. They look ceaselessly for somebody to torment. If we miss the fact that demons will interject their own ideas into our brains, if we assume that their lies are our own, then we will take ownership of those thoughts. We will let the demons and their lies fill our heads, and we will walk in defeat.

This is why it is imperative to monitor our thoughts. For the most part, people have no idea that they are sometimes not doing their own thinking. They fail to understand that Satan can intrude into one's consciousness.

A simple demonstration of this in the realm of the natural is the phenomenon of yawning. One person yawns and all of a sudden the people around that person start yawning, too. This is because the first yawn infiltrated the minds of the others. They did not suddenly decide to yawn. Something outside of them affected them.

Or take the analogy of weather. If it is gray outside because dark clouds block the sun, then we might feel gloomy or depressed—"under the weather." We feel better on a bright sunny day.

Put simply, we are affected by the environment. Something outside of us can have an impact on our behavior. We need to be aware of the fact that unclean spirits can indeed affect our lives—and they do it by putting thoughts and feelings, pictures and imagery into our heads.

Up to this point you have learned principles of self-deliverance that show you how to:

Close the doors through which demons gain access
Identify the presence of a demon in your life
Command the evil spirit to leave
Fill that space by confessing the positive
Grow in awareness that demons will try to return

You are well on the road to experiencing freedom!

In this chapter I want to explore more closely how demons try to sneak into our thoughts. Then I will show you a simple solution for dealing with them. This next stage of warfare is similar to commanding demons to leave; however, we will take it a step further.

Let's see what this looks like. Suppose you are gaining victory over a certain fear—perhaps the fear of running out of money. You now recognize when that demon is attacking you because you begin to have the old familiar thoughts that you will wind up destitute one day.

Your response is much like the steps we have already learned. You reject the lie quickly. You command that demon to leave you alone. Then you begin to speak the positive. You begin to quote God's Word over your life that He shall supply all your needs in Christ Jesus according to His riches. You declare that money is not something for you to worry about because God has promised to provide for you, even as He does the lilies of the field. You stay on the alert for the demon's return.

When you get dominance in one area of mental attack from demons, expect their strategy to shift.

Let's say that, in time, you have great success over that particular demon. You have trained yourself to reject his lie immediately, and the demon whose function it is to make you fearful about money cannot dominate your thoughts. This is victory! But this does not mean that Satan will never try to assault you again in a moment of weakness, or that he will stop looking for another way to get in.

Since fear has worked in the past, he uses the strategy of fear in a brand-new attack. He starts pummeling your mind with thoughts of fear of getting old and ending up in a nursing home in pain.

Now you have to learn to recognize that a demon is speaking this new lie to you, and you must respond with the same weapons. You reject the lie, you command the demon to leave you alone, and you fill your head with Scripture that counters thoughts of fear. You declare from the Word of God that He will never leave you or forsake you, even in your old age.

Self-deliverance is not like waving a magic wand. It is not something that is taken care of once and for all because someone drove a spirit off you. That can happen. I have seen people be completely freed from demonic attacks just that simply. But that is not the general model. Rather, we move step by step into a new place in the spiritual realm that the Lord opens for us, as we continue to fight and ascend in the heavenlies. We have to do warfare; we have to keep on fighting to maintain deliverance.

The Power of Deception

We read in Scripture that Satan "deceives the whole world" (Revelation 12:9). This is one of his primary ways of operating. Deception involves believing something that is not true—perceiving something in a wrong way.

We do not have to read very far in the Bible to see how Satan can use the power of deception. That is what led Adam and Eve to disobey God in the Garden of Eden: Satan came and spoke to them, and they were deceived.

The devil loves deception. It has worked for him against God's people for thousands of years.

What was behind the devil's deceptive words? Thoughts. In other words, Satan's infiltration of the human race began in the realm of thought. Behind the thought was a scheme to make Eve and her husband disobey God. He said to Eve, "Why don't you eat of the tree? God knows if you eat of it, you'll become like Him." It was a thought that deceived her. And Adam, who was standing there with her, also allowed his thinking to be warped. Their mental filtering systems did not perceive the lie, and their perspectives changed. They ate.

We just looked at God's words to Cain when the devil was tempting him: "Beware: Sin is crouching at the door. You must master it." Cain did not listen to God, and did not master the devil's desire for him. He let evil thoughts toward his brother, Abel, enter the door of his mind and, ultimately, demons of hatred and jealousy drove him to murder. Like Adam and Eve, he allowed his perspective of God, his family and his situation to be warped by demons.

Even King David, the great man of God, was deceived by Satan. First Chronicles 21:1 says: "Satan stood up against Israel and *moved David* to number Israel" (emphasis added).

David did not know that it was the devil who was moving him to take a census. He thought it was his own idea to count the number of people in Israel, so he had no resistance to it. It just seemed like a good idea to him to find out how strong his forces were for battle. No shield was up in his mind. He did not even consider coming against the idea. Rather than reject the sinful thought, he accepted it.

David was so deceived at this point, he would not listen to those who told him that this was a bad idea. His military commander expressed to him plainly that this would be sin and a cause of guilt for Israel, but David was adamant.

Now, David was not partnering with Satan consciously. He simply was not on guard against his enemy and paid dearly for it. Satan wanted to make Israel slip. He knew that if he could cause David to take an action that showed disbelief in God's promised protection for His people, then this action would bring an offense to and grieve God, which it did.

If David had looked at what was happening, he might have seen that his motive for the census was rooted in insecurity and pride, which opened the door for Satan to implant a demonic thought into his mind.

Thoughts from above, thoughts from below. You can tell the difference. Then you need to know what to do with them.

Satan's method of working has not changed over the millennia. This same being is still alive in the universe disguising himself as an angel of light today (see 2 Corinthians 11:14), and he is adept at coming to us in such a way that we mistake ungodly thoughts for our own. If we fail to recognize what is going on, we will not see that the devil is behind some of our thoughts even as he was behind Peter's thoughts when Peter tried to dissuade Jesus from going to the cross (see Matthew 16:23). Our perspective becomes warped, and we succumb to the deceit of the enemy.

Rethinking Our Thoughts

I was raised in a secular family that did not have a strong sense of morality in regard to premarital sex. In fact, my dad actually got a kick out of my exploits. When I was growing up, he would revel in my actions. He was proud of them.

After I was saved, I assumed that when I became a married adult all of my defiled sexual thinking patterns would automatically disappear. I felt fairly certain that I would be like Ward Cleaver driving my family around in a station wagon down apple tree–lined streets. (He was the wholesome dad on the television show *Leave It to Beaver* in the era of the late 1950s.)

But I found it was not that way. Deep thinking patterns and habits had been formed because of my own sin and because of the family lineage that I came out of. Even after deliverance from those spirits, it still took me many years to be able to separate what was God's will from a defiled conscience due to my earlier experiences in life.

When we find ourselves rooted in patterns of thinking from the realm of darkness, there is usually a process through which we are sanctified and delivered. We have to be cleansed from one degree of glory to the next degree of glory.

As I have said, discernment comes through maturation, and the more we practice the will of the Lord, the more discernment we have. And the more discernment we have, the more we can separate light from darkness and gain victory over the specific demonic thoughts that have become strongholds in our lives.

Scripture helps us to distinguish which thoughts are from the enemy and which are from God. James 3:17 says that thoughts from God are "first pure, then peaceable, gentle, reasonable, full of mercy and good fruits, unwavering, without hypocrisy."

Paul also wrote about what kinds of thoughts come from God:

Whatever is true, whatever is honorable, whatever is right, whatever is pure, whatever is lovely, whatever is of good repute, if there is any excellence and if anything worthy of praise, dwell on these things.

Philippians 4:8

We can know which thoughts are from God. The thoughts that produce the perspective of the Holy Spirit are coming from the Holy Spirit.

Regarding thoughts that are not from the Holy Spirit, the Bible says that there is a connection between the realm of the demonic and that part of the human nature that wants to sin. We know that we must reject demonic thoughts, but we also must reject all thoughts that come from our flesh; they have their basis in evil.

Paul explained it this way: "Set your mind on the things above," he says, "not on the things that are on earth" (Colossians 3:2). Some examples of earthly thoughts:

Immorality, impurity, passion, evil desire, and greed, which amounts to idolatry. For it is because of these things that the wrath of God will come upon the sons of disobedience. . . . Put them all aside: anger, wrath, malice, slander, and abusive speech from your mouth.

Colossians 3:5–6, 8

Demons work through fallen sinful human flesh. Fallen sinful human nature is sensual, for example, which can create a channel for a demon of lust. Fallen sinful human nature is prideful, which can create a channel for a demon of pride. Fallen sinful human nature is selfish, which can create a channel for a spirit of greed, etc.

Now, Paul lived what he taught. He did not receive every thought as his own. If a thought proceeded from the realm of the flesh, he did not receive it because he no longer identified himself with that fleshly part in him that was sinful. He dissociated himself from his flesh. He refused to own deceptive and destructive thoughts. He did not say, "I'm such a terrible person." Rather, he said, "I reject that thought, because it's not who I am."

This is important if we are going to maintain victory. Otherwise, every time we have a bad thought we are probably going to shame ourselves. Paul expressed it like this: "So now, no longer am I the one doing it, but sin which dwells in me. For I know that nothing good dwells in me, that is, in my flesh" (Romans 7:17–18).

Again, this is a crucial point. If Paul found himself doing something that he knew was wrong, his response was not, "I'm such a terrible, worthless, I'll-never-make-it person." Rather, he said, "I reject those sinful thoughts. They are not mine."

This is how we operate, whether the thought is from the realm of the demonic or the realm of the flesh. We reject all evil thoughts wherever they come from because we are justified, holy in Jesus. We have become the righteousness of God. As we walk in His light, we break the power of evil and put it under us and behind us.

Here and Now

One of the greatest ploys that Satan uses to deceive us is the illusion that we can get ahead in life by conquering something outside of ourselves. We think, *If I could just get that job promotion.... If I could just buy that house.... If I could just get that new dog.... If I could just marry that person.... If I could just have a baby.... If I could just get this much money in my retirement account.... If I could just get that guy back who beat me up when I was in the sixth grade....*

But you know what? When we get there we find that it was not the answer. We will never find peace by trying to overcome only in the external reality. Peace does not come from defeating somebody else. We find peace when we exercise authority over spiritual darkness and overcome it.

It is amazing to me that the people who wrote the Bible three thousand years ago had the answers for problems that we are still facing today. In the book of Proverbs, we read the words of Solomon. Scripture states that there never was anybody as wise before him and there never will be anybody as wise after him. Solomon said this: "He who is slow to anger is better than the mighty. And he who rules his spirit [is better than] he who captures a city" (Proverbs 16:32). Why is this true? Because that person is controlling himself.

We do not take dominion by controlling only the environment. Rather we begin to enter into freedom by controlling ourselves and ruling our own spirits. We walk in the assurance of peace when we recognize that our real enemy is wrapped around our own heads.

You and I need by the Spirit of God to break off the thoughts that are assaulting our minds. The primary battle is not "over there" somewhere; the battle is not first in our workplaces or homes. The battle is in the realm of our thoughts. The demons that we are dealing with are invisible spirits right here and right now.

> For though we walk in the flesh, we do not war according to the flesh, for the weapons of our warfare are not of the flesh, but divinely powerful for the destruction of fortresses. We are destroying speculations and every lofty thing raised up against the knowledge of God, and we are taking every thought captive to the obedience of Christ.
>
> 2 Corinthians 10:3–5

What is a fortress? A fortress is a place that is strongly fortified and often impenetrable. Demonic spirits can build fortresses in our minds. Demons usually work in teams and so have the reinforcements to construct these strongholds.

In other words, if you think about people who are angry, oftentimes they are angry because they are afraid. This means two spirits are at work. Think, for example, of the owner of a business who sees one of his employees slouching on the job. Sometimes rather than correct the employee by calmly explaining the repercussions if such bad behavior continues, the business owner responds with anger. Why is he angry? Because he is afraid of losing money in his business. This business owner first let in a demon of fear, and that demon made way for a demon of anger. They are now working in tandem, creating a demonic fortress.

That is why a lot of times in deliverance ministry it is beneficial to find the foundational demon. If we can break the grip of that demon, the other demons are going to go, too. In this case, if the demon of fear is dissipated, then there is no anger, because the spirit of anger is working off of the spirit of fear.

Fortresses are thought patterns that keep people trapped in bondage and darkness. They are speculations that exalt themselves above the knowledge of God. The good news is we can be free if we fight. When we keep our eyes on Jesus, we are warring in the Spirit—and we are warring with divinely inspired weapons.

James wrote: "Submit therefore to God. Resist the devil and he will flee from you" (4:7). When a demonic thought seeks to intrude into your space, and you recognize it and where it is coming from, you need to speak to it.

One Simple Command

As you grow in discernment and learn to distinguish the enemy's voice, you can resist him and send him away with one simple sentence.

"I reject you, Satan. Get out of my head!"

That is all you need to say. You might have to persevere in saying it over a period of time, but you will grow in boldness as you move in the authority and power of Jesus. You will become more and more confident that your warfare is effective.

So let's say that a thought comes into your mind of self-reproach, self-condemnation, self-rejection, hatred toward somebody, accusation toward somebody, fear or pride. As soon as the thought comes, you say: "I reject you, Satan. Get out of my head!" You do not necessarily have to say it in a loud voice, but you should say it as though you mean it, whether out loud or through your inner man.

You persist in this—not doing it one time, not doing it two times, not doing it three times to see if it works. Rather, you make up your mind that you are going to fight till you die. You are not going to surrender. You are not going to back off. You are going to fight until it is over, and you are going to win.

When you follow through with this, you are going to experience the demons weakening and disappearing. Thoughts that once plagued you no longer have access to you. You begin to sense that you are more aware of God's love, His peace and His power. And you are walking in greater freedom and greater consistency. Your ground is more stable. You begin to realize more and more, just as I do, the power that you have as a believer in Yeshua.

> *Every time a demonic thought comes, make up your mind to speak to it.*

I have found that by speaking to demonic spirits in this manner, something happens in the spirit realm. It is almost as if the devil is shocked. *Bam!* Oftentimes all of a sudden he is gone. Instantly I sense that my mind is free from the thought. It is clear and there is peace. Whether this happens immediately or takes a while, sooner or later it always works. Why? Because Jesus said, "I have given you authority over all the power of the enemy."

Examples for Practice

By the way, I prefer to use the word *reject* in this command rather than the word *rebuke*, which many are familiar with.

Reject is simply a more common word to work with and has the same meaning.

Let's see what this might look like. Suppose that a woman named Gina struggled with fear of people and fear of relationships for most of her life. She was able to identify those demons and command them to leave. The freedom she felt was exciting.

Within just a day or so, a familiar voice started whispering in her ear. But she understood these principles of recognizing and rejecting demonic thoughts. The battle in her head went something like this:

Gina, nobody wants to be around you.
"I reject you, Satan. Get out of my head!"

You know what? Those people were talking about you.
"I reject you, Satan. Get out of my head!"

You'll never make it around people.
"I reject you, Satan. Get out of my head!"

Nobody wants to be around you, Gina.
"I reject you, Satan. Get out of my head!"

You are really a loser.
"I reject you, Satan. Get out of my head!"

Gina was able to stand firm against the verbal assault as demons of rejection and failure tried to break down her defenses. After a while, those attacks stopped.

It is just that simple. We become aware that any thoughts destroying our peace are not our own thoughts. We realize that they are coming from the realm of darkness. We reject them. We might not be able to control whether or not birds fly over our heads, but we can control whether or not they nest there!

Let's look at another example.

Mark had been set free from the demonic stronghold that he could never do anything right. His self-image soared when he commanded those demonic trespassers to leave and they left. Mark was also prepared when the devil came again.

You can't do anything right.

Mark was ready: "I reject you, Satan. Get out of my head!"

You just mess everything up.
"I reject you, Satan. Get out of my head!"

You are probably a jinx!
"I reject you, Satan. Get out of my head!"

You are ruining everything again.
"I reject you, Satan. Get out of my head!"

Face the facts. You are a dull person.
"I reject you, Satan. Get out of my head!"

You are going to fail. You are not strong enough for this.
"I reject you, Satan. Get out of my head!"

Mark continued to walk in freedom. He worked at being conscious of what was traveling through his head, and he grew in confidence that he really had the victory. The enemy could not get back in! Praise God!

I hope that these two examples help you to see how this might work in your own life. You do not have to track down a deliverance minister to free you when the devil comes at you. You do not need someone who is experienced against the works of the devil to take command of the evil spirits that want to sabotage you. You can do it. John wrote: "You have an anointing from the Holy One" (1 John 2:20).

The apostle John also encouraged his readers with these words:

> Do not believe every spirit, but test the spirits to see whether they are from God. . . . You are from God, little children, and have overcome [the false spirits]; because greater is He who is in you than he who is in the world.
>
> 1 John 4:1, 4

You have the authority and power in Jesus to speak against the lies of the enemy and free yourself.

Protecting Your Thoughts for the Future

So let's review. The next time a demonic spirit tries to deceive you, what do you do? You recognize that it is a demon spirit. You acknowledge that the thought is not yours. You cast it down: "I reject you, Satan. Get out of my head!" You replace the thought of fear, lust, pride, accusation, judgment, inferiority and every other evil demonic thought with God's Word, which is truth.

The demonic thought is a lie. The only way to have victory over lies is to use God's Word authoritatively and aggressively. God's Word is living and active. By it Jesus created the world, cursed the fig tree, stilled the storm, healed the leper and delivered the demoniacs. Jesus is the Word. The Word lives in us. We confess the Word.

Our faith is not in whichever way we are feeling on a particular day. Our faith is in His Word. Jesus said, "It is the Spirit who gives life; the flesh profits nothing; the words that I have spoken to you are spirit and are life" (John 6:63).

Our words matter. Scripture says that we overcome by the word of our testimony (see Revelation 12:11). John also wrote:

> In the beginning was the Word, and the Word was with God, and the Word was God. He was in the beginning with God. . . . In Him was life, and the life was the Light of men. The Light shines in the darkness, and the darkness did not comprehend [overpower] it.
>
> John 1:1–2, 4–5

There are only two choices. If we neglect to take hold of Yeshua's Word, there will be another word filling us. We can be sure that Satan is still crouching at the door, hoping to devour us. He never gives up. Scripture says, for instance, that after Moses died, the devil was actually fighting the archangel Michael for his body (see Jude 9). The devil desired Moses, and he desires you and me, too.

Jesus said seven times in the opening chapters of Revelation that in order to inherit the ecstasies of heaven we have to overcome. In order to overcome and have the freedom that is ours in Him, we must press in, press on and fight to win.

Are we going to be aggressive in spirit and choose to replace lies with God's truth? Are we going to follow our

Captain into warfare with the devil? Or are we going to be passive and be swept away?

Every single one of us has the responsibility to choose. You cannot do for me what only I can do for me, and I cannot do for you what only you can do for you. You and I are responsible for what we are thinking. We are responsible for taking authority over the devil.

Each one of us will stand before God. I want to stand there as one who has overcome. To do this, I have to fight just as you do.

We can win this battle. Let's look now at how we can be strong and hold the course. Spiritual warfare is difficult, but Jesus knows everything we need to be successful. He will help us fight until the fight is over.

7

When the Going Gets Rough

In the opening chapter of this book, I mentioned the story of Israel's entering her Promised Land as an analogy for our work of self-deliverance. Even though God gave the land of milk and honey to His children, they still had to engage in warfare to take possession. They did this by persisting in battle after battle, driving out the inhabitants systematically and ruthlessly.

The stories of Israel's ancient warfare are not just Old Testament history; they are symbols of spiritual reality. Paul tells us specifically in 1 Corinthians 10:11 that "these things"—the lessons from Israel's struggles—"happened to them as an example, and they were written for our instruction." Events in Israel's history apply to our lives today.

Everything in the Hebrew Bible is a physical, natural, flesh-and-blood symbolic foreshadowing of the days we are now living in. The story of Moses building the Tabernacle, for example, shows us a type of the spiritual Tabernacle in the heavenly places. Israel's institution of holy days represents Yeshua's life, death and soon return. This is why it is so important to know the Hebrew Bible. Without knowledge of it, we end up with a much weaker understanding of who God is.

Israel's effort to take possession of her inheritance, then, was a specific prophetic foreshadowing of our entering into the fullness of our inheritance in Jesus. Just as Israel drove out the Amorites, the Hittites and the Jebusites, so we need to drive out our enemies in order to take possession of the abundant life the Spirit offers us.

We can claim the inheritance that is ours, but this is not something that happens overnight or without cost and effort. In this chapter we look at principles that help us stay the course.

Winning Takes Time

A primary lesson for us as we observe Israel's taking possession of her Promised Land is this: Our battle against darkness is won as we persevere.

There are going to be days when the devil turns up the heat against you, leaving you just about ready to quit. You are doing your best to grow the fruit of the Spirit in your life—peace, patience, self-control—but instead of making headway, you feel stuck. It seems as though you will never win the battle against the evil you are facing.

Evil spirits are going to keep on opposing, resisting and seeking to torment you—even when you give your best effort. If discouragement comes, you have two choices. You can stop and say, "This doesn't work," or you can keep on fighting. Obviously, the right choice is to stay on the offensive and to keep fighting. Continue to take authority over demonic thoughts whenever they come. Stay the course. Speak the truth of Scripture.

It might seem as though it is taking forever, but you *will* begin to feel fortified internally. Whether it takes weeks or months or years, you will find yourself getting stronger and stronger inside. Armor is fitting into place to help protect you. Soon those spirits will not be able to bother you as they once did, and the battle will be won.

Look specifically at what God told Israel about her enemies: He said, "I will drive them out before you *little by little*, until you become fruitful and take possession of the land" (Exodus 23:30, emphasis added).

This is an important verse for us in the realm of spiritual warfare and self-deliverance. I think I can say that many of the victories I have experienced happened little by little. This is not to take away from the fact that God is gracious and sometimes delivers people with a seeming snap of His fingers. I know several people who have been delivered from smoking in a moment, just like *that*. They never had the desire to smoke again. But most people get delivered by hanging on to Jesus, staying committed, trusting, praying. And little by little, they get free.

> *Is your battle for freedom heating up? Remember what Scripture says about this as you move forward.*

We must never doubt that we will win our inheritance in Jesus. As we engage in warfare and call out to God in our weakness, little by little the strength comes, the defense comes, the revelation comes. And more and more we enter into freedom. That is why Jesus said, "If you *continue* in My word." What is that word *continue*? It is a process. Every day. "If you *continue* in My word, then . . . you will know the truth, and the truth will make you free. . . . [And] if the Son makes you free, you will be free indeed" (John 8:31–32, 36, emphasis added).

Sometimes God snaps His fingers against evil; sometimes He strengthens your armor.

As you continue on your journey of self-deliverance, I want you to be aware of a demonic tactic. First, demons put into your mind a fearful, evil thought. Then they put into your mind the idea that if you try to conquer that evil thought, the very thing you fear most will come about.

Let me give you an example. One of the demonic attacks against me using this double whammy was the fear that harm would come to my daughters. The devil tormented me with fear in that area. Then, in addition, I was terrified subconsciously that if I addressed that particularly frightening thought, it would happen. The devil was keeping me in bondage by making me afraid of what would occur if I looked at my area of fear.

For a long time in my life I did not know any better than to live in defeat. I yielded to the evil spirits and got along as best I could with the fears and trials. I was playing right into their hands.

But as God began to show me what was going on, I began to resist. I learned how to speak God's Word out loud and confess God's protection of my children. (Once again, confession can be made literally through your physical mouth or from your inner man. Both means are effective in the spiritual realm.)

I held tightly to this Scripture: "Resist the devil and he will flee from you" (James 4:7). As I began to take rightful authority over evil spirits, they lost their hold. They disconnected. They fell away. And God brought me into a new place—a place of fruitfulness as I moved into the abundant life the Spirit of God offers.

Many give up or refuse to engage in spiritual warfare because they do not want to look at something that makes them afraid, but this simply gives demons more freedom to plot against them. That area you dread facing might be the most crucial area in which you need to fight. Satan wants you to cower from demonic torment. But, as you realize by now, if you fail to look at thoughts that come from demons, then there can be no positive outcome.

If we think that one command to the devil and his demons is going to free us completely from every assault forever, then we are setting ourselves up for disillusionment and defeat. Self-deliverance is a process of walking in the revelation and light that the Holy Spirit continues to give us. We get freer and freer and stronger and stronger as we put God's truth and principles into practice in our lives.

So we take Exodus 23:30 to heart: "I will drive them out before you little by little, until you become fruitful and take possession of the land." You start out knowing that you are going to be driving these powers out from your life progressively, that it is going to happen little by little, and that as you move forward, you are going to become fruitful. You are going to take possession of the abundant life that God's Word and Jesus promise!

Moving Mountains

Scripture gives us another powerful analogy in our battle against evil spirits. This one is from the New Testament.

> When they came to the crowd, a man came up to Jesus, falling on his knees before Him and saying, "Lord, have mercy on my son, for he is a lunatic and very ill; for he often falls into the fire and often into the water. I brought him to Your disciples, and they could not cure him." . . . And Jesus rebuked [the demon], and the demon came out of him, and the boy was cured at once.
>
> Then the disciples came to Jesus privately and said, "Why could we not drive it out?" And He said to them, "Because of the littleness of your faith; for truly I say to you, if you have faith the size of a mustard seed, you will say to this mountain, 'Move from here to there,' and it will move; and nothing will be impossible to you. But this kind does not go out except by prayer and fasting."
>
> Matthew 17:14–16, 18–21

Here we see that Jesus was teaching His disciples about the effect of faith: It can move mountains.

Have you ever taken this literally and wondered why no one has ever stood in front of a mountain and commanded it to fall into the sea—and succeeded? Why no one has ever relocated Mount St. Helens or Mount Everest?

It is because Jesus was using a parable here, a figurative illustration. He was alluding to the demonic realm. The mountains that He was speaking of were demonic strongholds and forces of darkness that oppose God's Spirit.

Jesus shows the correct way of moving mountains. But let us first ask, What, exactly, is a mountain?

When the disciples asked why they could not drive the demon out, Jesus said that if they would fast and pray, they would have the necessary faith to say to the mountain, "Move from here to there," and it would move. Notice that there was a cost: They had to fast and pray.

We looked earlier at Jesus' example of fasting in the wilderness—how He chose to place Himself in a voluntary position of weakness in order to be made strong in the Spirit. Fasting and prayer play a significant role in entering into freedom. We need to be sensitive when the Holy Spirit is saying to us, *You know what? I don't want you leaning into that thing so heavily. I want you to step away from that thing and come with Me to a lonely place for a while. Realize that you depend on Me.*

Fasting can take many forms. We need to respond to whatever it is that the Holy Spirit calls us to fast from in order to build our faith. Maybe it is a spiritual fast to come away from everything and sit at Jesus' feet as we wait on God. Maybe it is a physical fast from food, television, the Internet. Whatever form it takes, fasting strengthens us in our resistance to evil and builds us up in the Spirit of God. Fasting is a powerful statement that we are not going to give up when it comes to resisting evil. Rather, we are going to look to God to strengthen us in our weakness.

I want to tell you about a fasting experience I had, and how the Holy Spirit drove home to me the idea that taking the easy way when the going gets rough will rob you and me of victory.

> Fasting makes the statement that you are serious about your freedom, and not going to look for an easy way out.

I had been praying for about a year for Jesus to increase my sense of peace. This was my focused and concentrated prayer. Then I had an encounter with the Lord. It was the most emotionally rich encounter I have ever experienced. It was not at the same level of revelation that I have received in some areas, but I have not had an encounter with Him that has had higher emotional impact. In other words, I literally *felt* Him.

One night while I was asleep, I found myself standing in a beautifully lush forest. Every spot around me was overflowing with thick green plants. Surrounding this forest were huge boulders. These rock formations made the forest seem secluded and hidden. There was lush green growth on the boulders as well.

As I stood in wonder at such lushness and richness, I began to experience billows of God's peace rolling over my soul. The peace came like great waves pouring over me. It was truly supernatural, and unlike anything I had ever experienced before.

I then sensed the Spirit of God leading me deeper into the heart of the forest, where I saw a simple wooden picnic table. I knew that this table represented a place of even greater experience in the Spirit, a place of union with Him. In the book of Revelation, Jesus offers to dine with us (see Revelation 3:20). I was being invited to join Him, dine with Him and experience Him in His fullness.

Suddenly something unexpected entered the picture. A slice of pizza appeared, and it was about two inches from my nose. I was instantly captivated by this pizza. It was the most aromatic pizza I have ever smelled in my life. The steaming melted cheese and herbs were tantalizing.

At that point I became utterly double-minded. On the one hand, I wanted to yield to the Spirit of God and be drawn to His table deeper in the forest. I knew that if I did, I would experience more of His supernatural presence and peace.

Yet, on the other hand, the pizza aroused my flesh. I was ravenous for that slice of pizza. I really wanted it.

I knew it was one or the other. I could yield to the Spirit of God or I could satisfy my senses.

But then I had the thought that maybe I could strike a deal. Maybe it would be all right to have some pizza and *then* go enjoy the rich, deep presence of the Spirit of God.

As soon as I had that thought, the encounter with the Lord ended. I awoke instantly. I got out of bed and got on my knees asking God to forgive me. I could not believe it. I had been longing and praying for a year for more of His peace, and right when He offered it to me, I traded it for the pleasure of the flesh.

I begged God to let me have another try. I said, "Lord, I'm going back to bed now. Please come and visit me again and give me another chance."

I went back to bed, but the experience did not return.

When I got up the next morning, I sat down on my couch and began to talk to the Lord about what had happened. I asked Him, "Lord, where did the pizza come from? Did You put it there to test me? Or did the devil put it there to rob me of an experience with You?"

As I meditated on this, I came to believe that even if the devil had interjected the pizza thought to make me fall, God is still in charge of my life. I sensed His perfect ability to use everything that happens to me as part of His good plan for me. He causes everything to work together for the good of His children, as Romans 8:28 promises.

So then I pondered this further and asked, "God, why did You want the pizza to be part of this experience? Was it to become a lesson for me?"

This, I felt, was the answer. I believe that the Lord wanted me to see that in order for us to have more of His Holy Spirit, to have more of His peace and to grow in the kind of faith that will bring us into victory in the spirit realm in heavenly places, we need to deny the flesh.

When we fast and pray to make ourselves hungry for His Spirit, we will receive more of His presence in our lives. When we choose not to follow the easy path of giving in to the flesh, but deny ourselves in order to receive more of Him, we will be nourished by the Spirit and built up in our faith in Jesus.

We have to be serious about getting free. If we are iffy about staying in the battle and not committed to winning it, we will not move in to our full inheritance. But if we yield to the Lord and follow Him, we will receive the power we need to gain the next victory.

This is not intended to put us under judgment; this is simply meant to help us understand persistence and the need to get tough. Part of getting free means recognizing that the Holy Spirit requires self-discipline. We need to trust and obey. As we obey Him in simple areas that bring us into deliverance, we will find our confidence growing. If we persist, we will see that we can trust Him to help us move the demonic mountains that stand in our way, and we will enter into greater and greater levels of freedom and victory.

Seamless Prayer

Persistence is born out of and sustained by a relationship with God. In other words, true freedom in Jesus is a lifestyle. Prayer is not something that we do for a certain number of minutes each day—and then consider ourselves done. As in my picture of the lush forest, we move deeper and deeper into the place that the Holy Spirit is calling us to so that Jesus can turn our weakness into His strength. He builds our faith so we can break out of bondage and into our inheritance.

The goal is to be in constant communion with God. "Pray without ceasing," Paul wrote in 1 Thessalonians 5:17. In John 11 we read that before Jesus raised Lazarus from the dead, He raised His eyes to the Father and prayed, "Father, I thank You that You have heard me. I knew that You always hear Me; but because of the people standing around I said it, so that they may believe that You sent Me" (verses 41–42).

Jesus was in constant prayer. His walk on earth could be considered a seamless prayer dialogue with His Father. He prayed ceaselessly.

The concepts of self-deliverance that we are learning must be mixed with a lifestyle of prayer and fasting. We need to talk to God more than we talk with even our dearest family members or friends. We cling to God. We call out to Him in our weakness. As we do so, He strengthens us, and we can stand with assurance in the war against evil.

The point is that prayer is constant communion. It is not only talking with God but also cultivating a supernatural sense of His presence with us. This is the goal, and the surest way through the hard times.

Good People in Hard Places

One of the roughest areas for most people to get through in warfare is staying close to God when we see things happening that we do not understand. It is easy to trust God when all is going well; it is more likely that we doubt God's provision and care when we see bad things happening to good people.

There was a time in my life when I looked around and saw good people facing really hard battles. It was getting difficult to see evidence of God's goodness in the lives of faithful people who served Him with loving hearts. I grew more and more discouraged. Everywhere I turned I saw pain and heartache and failure. I would read the words of Psalm 91 and think, *Lord, where are You in this person's life? Where are Your promises? Why are things going so wrong for this one?*

I had no clue how to deal with this apparent discrepancy between what God's Word says we should be experiencing as His people and what many who seemed to be in personal relationship with Him were *actually* experiencing. Because I did not know how to reconcile the discrepancy, I basically tried to ignore it. Then the Lord showed me something.

On a particularly cold and icy winter night, I was ministering with a team in our congregation. After the service, when most of the people were heading for their cars, a member of the team came rushing back inside saying that his wife had fallen in the parking lot and was in a lot of pain. He asked us to come pray for her.

In my heart, the question I had been struggling with reached a tipping point. Silently but with great inner turmoil, I asked the Lord about this. I said, *Lord, this lady has just finished ministering for You! I know that You cause all things to work together for good, but couldn't You have kept her from falling?*

In my discouragement over the next couple of days I asked Him why the angels were not protecting His people. I poured out my grief that only a few of His children seemed to be walking in the promises that are ours. I begged Him for an answer.

I can see now that at the heart of my prayer was my fear that God was not really trustworthy. He had not kept my team member from falling; how then could I trust Him to help me? I was very sad and disheartened. I said to Father God: "Until You give me an answer, as to why so many people who say they know You and appear to love You are failing and falling, I am not going to be able to trust You for myself. I need to understand this, Father God, because I am stuck. If You are not protecting and blessing them, how can I trust and believe that You will protect and bless me? Please help me understand this."

At that point, I just waited on God for an answer. Deep in my heart I expected Him to answer me. And I also knew that I could not move forward in my relationship with Him until He did.

In another day or so, I was driving along in my SUV when the Holy Spirit spoke to me deep within my heart. He said: *The reason you are seeing My people failing and falling is because they are not trusting Me.*

These words were spoken to me so clearly, I knew I was hearing His voice.

Within the message, He gave me a revelation of the word *trusting*. I heard the sound of the word *trusting*, but it had the meaning of "clinging." He was imparting to me His own heart's desire for His people to *cling to Him* so that He can impart the protection and the sufficiency of Himself that He longs to give. Again, this is why Jesus said, "Blessed are the poor in spirit, for theirs is the Kingdom of God." He works most fully in our lives when we cling to Him with our whole heart.

This, I realized, is one of the goals of a lifestyle of fasting and prayer. Remember how Paul asked Jesus to remove the "thorn" that was imbedded painfully in his flesh. The Lord responded with the message that Paul needed to turn to Him, to *cling* to Him more closely, because in Paul's own weakness caused by the thorn, the Lord's strength would be made most evident.

Keep Going!

Keep going. Continue to press forward, and do not stop when the going gets rough. Everyone can get free. Jesus' death, burial, resurrection, ascension to heaven and the giving of His Spirit make it possible for all of us who believe in Him to gain victory.

Jesus encourages us to be persistent in our fight with evil. He also has much to say about being aggressive. This takes us to our next teaching of Jesus about spiritual warfare, which is this: "Violent men take [the Kingdom of heaven] by force" (Matthew 11:12). What did Jesus mean by this statement? Does violence have a place in the Kingdom? Let's explore this and apply it to all we have learned about self-deliverance from evil spirits.

8

The Violent Take the Kingdom

When I was about eight years old, a boy in our neighborhood would throw rocks at me whenever I walked by his house. I was afraid of him. Who wants to get hit with a rock?

I went crying to my dad about it, and he said, "You're going to have to face that kid."

I took his words to heart. I charged outside, went over to his house, found him on his front lawn, and *bam!* One punch and he never threw a rock at me again.

Now this is not a great lesson in human relations, but it works when we apply it to our fight against the forces of darkness. As we have learned, power and authority exercised with persistence is the only language that the devil understands.

We need to grasp the concept of holy violence, and to develop the boldness it takes to use spiritual aggression effectively against the enemy. God wants to teach us about this in order to help us move forward into our promised inheritance.

This is the way Jesus lived. He was aggressive against darkness. First John 3:8 says: "The Son of God appeared for this purpose, to destroy the works of the devil." He did not come to tolerate the works of evil; He came to destroy them.

Scripture teaches that the words holy *and* violence *belong in the same sentence when you are battling demons.*

Satan does not go away if we address him—even persistently—with a passive spirit. Satan does not go away if we ask him politely to leave. Satan responds to a holy resolve. Think of the righteous anger that Jesus showed when He went after the buyers and sellers in the Temple. He was enraged, overturning the tables and driving the commerce out of God's house.

That was holy violence, and that is what is necessary in self-deliverance. As we walk forward into victory against evil, the enemy will use every force he can to block us. Jesus wants His followers to continue on the offensive. He wants us to be strong in the use of godly power in order to claim our inheritance in His Kingdom.

We see from the New Testament that Jesus trained His disciples to engage in holy violence. We see, as well, that this teaching fills the Hebrew Bible, such as when God commanded the children of Israel to wipe out the nations He was driving out before them:

> "When the LORD your God brings you into the land where you are entering to possess it, and clears away many

nations before you, the Hittites and the Girgashites and the Amorites . . . and when the LORD your God delivers them before you and you defeat them, then you shall utterly destroy them. You shall make no covenant with them and show no favor to them."

Deuteronomy 7:1–2

Remember, the historical accounts recorded in the Old Testament serve as a physical image of a greater reality in the Spirit. Let's increase our understanding of what it means to "utterly destroy" our enemy with holy violence.

Embracing Kingdom Violence

Jesus was specific about our need to exercise holy passion against evil. When John the Baptist was imprisoned by Herod, Jesus paid him this tribute:

> "Truly I say to you, among those born of women there has not arisen anyone greater than John the Baptist! Yet the one who is least in the kingdom of heaven is greater than he. From the days of John the Baptist until now the kingdom of heaven suffers violence, *and violent men take it by force*."

Matthew 11:11–12, emphasis added

Look in particular at these words: *the kingdom of heaven suffers violence, and violent men take it by force.* We know that the Kingdom is the inheritance of God's children, but what exactly did Jesus mean by saying that the violent take it by force? This seems like a perplexing statement from the Prince of Peace, but not if we understand the war we are in.

There are two messages here. On the one hand, Jesus was saying that people who are possessed by violent spirits of darkness will attack the Kingdom of God.

Let's examine this through the light of biblical history. Pharaoh of Egypt commanded the deaths of all male Hebrew children (see Exodus 1:15–16) in an attempt to destroy God's deliverer for His people (Moses). When Jesus was born, King Herod tried to murder Him by ordering the slaughter of all the male children in and around Bethlehem under the age of two (see Matthew 2:16). John the Baptist was beheaded (see Matthew 14:10). Judas betrayed Jesus to those who sought to kill Him. John 13:27 says that "Satan . . . entered into" Judas. Finally, in the book of Revelation, as we look into the spirit world, we see the dragon trying to swallow Jesus when He was born (see Revelation 12:13–16).

> *The Kingdom of God is the inheritance of every believer. And like the children of Israel, you have to fight for your promised land.*

These are all examples of how the kingdom of darkness attacks the Kingdom of God. We are never going to be free in this lifetime from the reality that we have an enemy. In fact, the more tightly we cling to Jesus and gain ground, the more viciously the enemy will sometimes attack *because of* our forward progress. He wants to stop you and me from taking the Kingdom. You can probably attest to this.

I know in my own life there are times that as soon as I take a step forward in my relationship with Jesus, I have to deal with a stronger demonic attack. One time as I was making progress in my relationship with the Lord, I was attacked violently at night by an evil spirit.

This happened about three years after I had first come to know the Lord. I had been pondering the verse in the book of Hebrews that says God "is a rewarder of those who seek Him" (Hebrews 11:6). So I decided one day that I was going to spend all the next day seeking God. I got up in the morning, and all I did for about fourteen hours that entire day was pray and listen to worship music.

I remember vividly, as I walked into my bedroom that night, how excited I was thinking about the great reward that was coming to me. I was thinking about how I had spent all day seeking God, and the fact that the Bible promises God's reward for those who seek Him. I went to sleep, and I cannot explain what happened, except to say that I was attacked in my sleep by the most violent spirit that I have ever encountered. I felt as though I were a dodge ball being slammed against the four walls of my bedroom— *bam! bam! bam! bam!* It was definitely supernatural, and it was definitely demonic.

The next morning I was thoroughly shaken by what had happened. Then a thought that was birthed in fear began to creep into my mind. It said: *You had better not seek God so aggressively or this is going to happen to you again.*

Though I was a new believer, I knew where that thought was coming from. The enemy wanted to make me afraid that he would continue to harm me if I kept going forward. I rejected the thought immediately. It was a battle, but I was persistent and the demon's hold broke.

My point here is that just as the devil tried to kill Israel's deliverer in Egypt, and just as the dragon tried to kill Jesus when He was born, so evil will attack us sometimes when we are moving forward in our walks with God. The Kingdom of heaven suffers violence from attacks of evil. God gave Israel the Promised Land but the people still had to fight a strong enemy. And so it is in our lives today.

The second message from the words of Jesus in His statement that *the kingdom of heaven suffers violence, and violent men take it by force* is that in order to take possession of the Kingdom of God, we need to have within us a spirit of sanctified holy violence.

This is not the type of violence that is bred in darkness. Jesus was not talking about the type of violent spirit that resides in the murderers within our prison systems who have not given their lives to Him. Rather, He was describing a holy resolve, a righteous aggressive spirit against evil. The Kingdom of God will be inherited by everyone who is ruthless in his or her resolve to take hold of it.

Jesus offers us the gift of forgiveness by the power of His shed blood, but He wants even more for us. He wants to make us *free indeed*. The Kingdom is ours. It is our inheritance. But we need to learn that it is necessary to fight and to fight violently in order to take it. We need to have a spiritual resolve against the enemy just as Jesus had, who "appeared for this purpose, to destroy the works of the devil."

This does not mean that we no longer try to exhibit all the fruit of the Holy Spirit—love, joy, peace, patience and so on. But it does mean that we *must* use righteous anger against the devil.

In other words, "turning the other cheek" does not suggest that we let an enemy tear down our homes and beat up our families. Turning the other cheek is a moral response. If somebody does something evil, we live above it. We do not respond by going down to his or her level. We return good for evil.

But there are times that we also defend ourselves. At one point Jesus told Peter to put away his sword (see John 18:11), but at another point He said: "'Now . . . whoever has no sword is to sell his coat and buy one.' . . . They said, 'Lord, look, here are two swords.' And He said to them, 'It is enough'" (Luke 22:36, 38).

The Target Matters

A key to dealing with defiled spirits with holy and righteous anger is taking care not to express a spirit of anger in an unrighteous way. Paul wrote: "Be angry, and yet do not sin" (Ephesians 4:26). In other words, aggression is a godly thing as long as we aim it at the right target. This means redirecting the anger we feel toward people who are rude, or the frustration we feel when we are in a hurry to check out at the grocery store and someone is slowing down the line.

It takes discipline to stop pouring out our frustration in the wrong way—on our kids, our friends, our spouses, our employers, the car in front of us, God, the weather. But when we do, we are going to see changes.

Holy violence is a matter of redirecting our thinking to something like this: "Lord, my fight is not against flesh and blood. This situation is not my real problem. My real problem is the spiritual warfare that I am in. There is something else tormenting me and making me mad. Father, help me release appropriate anger at the one who is really making me feel this way—an evil spirit of darkness."

I saw my wife, Cynthia, do this just the other day. She dropped a really big smoothie drink that she had just made. It had all kinds of that good stuff in it—kale and whatnot. She had just made it, and it slipped out of her hand onto the floor. Green liquid slopped everywhere.

In the moments that followed, Cynthia was silent, staring at the pool around her feet. I happened to be nearby at the time, and wondered what she was thinking. I said, "Doesn't that make you mad?"

She said, "Yes, but. . . ."

And then she shrugged her shoulders and went and got the mop.

She knew that she had a choice to make. She could yell and scream and vent her frustration. But, really, at what? What good would that do? That would not be God's direction for her in that situation.

We need to resist taking out our anger on the wrong targets, and learn to release it appropriately where it should be released—at the evil spirits that try to keep us from gaining the Kingdom.

Think about what it feels like when you are really mad. That is the feeling you want to have against the devil. If you use that feeling in the Spirit of God against the enemy, instead of against people, the enemy is going to run from you. He is going to be afraid to touch you!

I have also noticed that when I hold my anger and keep myself from releasing it in the wrong way and at the wrong target, there is a greater anointing on me when I am ministering.

I experienced this just recently. In the middle of a service, I ran into all types of PowerPoint and sound system challenges. This was one more instance in what had been ongoing agitation with the electronics. It was very frustrating for me as I felt the weight of leading the service, and wanting the momentum to continue, but having to stop and try to help those who were doing their best with the balky equipment.

Frankly I was mad. But I recognized the true target and did not let that anger get directed toward the ones who simply could not get the electronics working. I went ahead and ministered in spite of the frustration inside. As a result, I sensed great authority on me. Somehow God transformed that struggle, that self-discipline required in being angry but not sinning, into anointing on me as I ministered to His people.

God's View of His Enemies

Earlier we examined Israel's battle to enter into their inheritance from their perspective. Let's now examine this same experience from God's point of view. Here are some Scriptures that reveal the mind of God.

In Exodus 23:31 the Lord said:

"I will fix your boundary from the Red Sea to the sea of the Philistines, and from the wilderness to the River Euphrates; for I will deliver the inhabitants of the land into your hand, and you will drive them out before you."

In Numbers 33:51–53 the Lord said to Moses:

"Speak to the sons of Israel and say to them, 'When you cross over the Jordan into the land of Canaan, then you shall drive out all the inhabitants of the land from before you, and destroy all their figured stones, and destroy all their molten images and demolish all their high places; and you shall take possession of the land and live in it, for I have given the land to you to possess it.'"

In Deuteronomy 7:2 the Lord said:

"When the LORD your God delivers them before you and you defeat them, then you shall utterly destroy them. You shall make no covenant with them and show no favor to them."

In Deuteronomy 9:3 the Lord said:

"Know therefore today that it is the LORD your God who is crossing over before you as a consuming fire. He will destroy them and He will subdue them before you, so that you may drive them out and destroy them quickly just as the LORD has spoken to you."

This kind of destruction might seem hard, even cruel, but listen: God had a purpose in this. If the Israelites had been soft on the enemy—soft on the Amorites, soft on the Jebusites, soft on the Canaanites—then those squatters would have hindered His people from living fully for Him. The enemy needed to be driven out completely for God's people to receive all that He desired for them.

The deeper spiritual reality of this passage suggests once again that we can show no mercy in our battles against evil. In order for us as the children of God to take full possession of our inheritance, we need to drive out the enemy *ruthlessly*.

Unless we develop an aggressive spirit against darkness and challenge it and hate it, then we are going to miss a great deal that God has for us. The enemy is *always* going to try to hinder us from God's purposes. We need to recognize this and *hate* him with holy hatred.

Sometimes we have trouble connecting the term *hatred* to God, but be assured, Scripture makes clear that God hates certain things:

> There are six things which the LORD *hates*, yes, seven which are an abomination to Him: haughty eyes, a lying tongue, and hands that shed innocent blood, a heart that devises wicked plans, feet that run rapidly to evil, a false witness who utters lies, and one who spreads strife among brothers.
>
> Proverbs 6:16–19, emphasis added

Wisdom teaches that "the fear of the LORD is to hate evil" (Proverbs 8:13). David, a man after God's own heart, wrote: "Do I not hate those who hate You, O LORD? And do I not loathe those who rise up against You? I hate them with the utmost hatred; they have become my enemies" (Psalm 139:21–22). God also made clear to the Israelites that He hates the abominable acts of idol worshipers (see Deuteronomy 12:31) and their detestable idols (see Deuteronomy 16:22).

If you fail to have an aggressive spirit against darkness, you are going to miss many of your Kingdom blessings.

Sometimes God's ways seem hard, but they are necessary in order to take possession of the Kingdom. This is the reason Jesus responded the way He did to the man who wanted to follow Him, but asked that he might first be allowed to bury his father (see Matthew 8:21–22).

Suppose you said to me, "Rabbi, I'd love to be at the service tonight, but I've got to go and bury my dad."

I wonder what you would think of me if I said to you, "Listen, brother, listen, sister, you let the dead bury the dead. You'd better be there tonight, or you're not coming back."

What would you think? But that is what Jesus said. He told the man: "Whoever begins to follow Me and then looks back is not worthy of Me. Let the dead bury the dead. You follow Me, and then go preach the Gospel everywhere."

Do you see His holy spiritual resolve against the weakness of the flesh and against human emotions that get in the way of our taking the Kingdom of God? We cannot be controlled by the people or events around us. We cannot be controlled by human emotion. We cannot be controlled by sentimentalism. We cannot be controlled by the enemy.

We need to get radical for Jesus. His ways are above our ways, even as heaven is higher than the earth.

We Are Not Alone

When the children of Israel marched into the Promised Land, they engaged themselves heart and soul in the process. They were fighting for their lives. They had their swords; they had their armor. With blood, sweat and tears they put themselves 100 percent into the process of driving out their enemies.

And as they moved forward with holy resolve, something supernatural started to happen: God started fighting with them, supernaturally backing them up. Look again at Deuteronomy 9:3 (emphasis added):

> "Know therefore today that it is the LORD your God who is crossing over before you as a consuming fire. *He will destroy them* and He will subdue them before you, *so that you may drive them out* and destroy them quickly just as the LORD has spoken to you."

We have to be fully engaged, but God does not leave us alone in the battle. God is not simply telling us to do something and then leaving. He will work with us supernaturally and empower us to be victorious.

This is good news!

The apostle Paul illustrated this same concept: "By the grace of God I am what I am, and His grace toward me did not prove vain; but I labored even more than all of them, yet not I, but the grace of God with me" (1 Corinthians 15:10).

We are engaged in warfare against the devil. We work, battle and struggle, but we are not alone. You and I are going to be victorious because God is fighting with us on our behalf. We put forth the full effort while recognizing that God is doing the empowering. He is going before us and giving us the success.

Fighting with Passion

Another Old Testament passage helps us understand the necessity of holy violence in order to take the Kingdom.

This powerful lesson is given in 2 Kings 13. We read that the great prophet Elisha had served as mentor to Joash, king of Israel, and now Elisha was about to die. Joash loved and revered this powerful man of God, and was not sure how to face the future without him.

Joash was despairing at the thought of the ongoing warfare that Israel would be facing. So Elisha took one last opportunity before his death to prepare the king for the war ahead. Elisha gave him these instructions.

> Elisha said to him, "Take a bow and arrows." So he took a bow and arrows. Then he said to the king of Israel, "Put your hand on the bow." And he put his hand on it, then Elisha laid his hands on the king's hands.
>
> 2 Kings 13:15–16

By this act Elisha was transferring anointing to Joash.

> He said, "Open the window toward the east," and he opened it. Then Elisha said, "Shoot!" And he shot. And he said, "The LORD's arrow of victory, even the arrow of victory over Aram; for you will defeat the Arameans at Aphek until you have destroyed them." Then he said, "Take the arrows," and he took them. And he said to the king of Israel, "Strike the ground," and he struck it three times and stopped. So the man of God was angry with him and said, "You should have struck five or six times, then you would have struck Aram until you would have destroyed it. But now you shall strike Aram only three times."
>
> verses 17–19

What happened here? Elisha was preparing the king for victory over Israel's enemies, but the king secured only partial success because he lacked the holy spiritual resolve and violence required to be effective.

He had shot the arrow of victory, but when Elisha told him to strike the ground with the arrows, he struck the ground only three times, showing a lack of passion about the ultimate defeat of the Arameans. If he had put more into it, more force, more passion, more holy anger, he would never have had trouble with that enemy again. If he had struck five or six times, he would have been able to destroy his enemy completely.

Training for War

We hear little in the Church today about the warrior spirit that is needed in our lives in order to take possession of the Kingdom. We seem to be in a trend of passivity in which we drink cappuccinos while sitting in our pews listening to the sermon. There is a focus on making people feel good and comfortable. We fail to understand that we are in a war, and that we must be disciplined and trained.

David wrote these words: "Blessed be the LORD, my rock, who *trains my hands for war, and my fingers for battle*" (Psalm 144:1, emphasis added). Paul declared in Ephesians 6 that we should arm ourselves. We are not fully armed if we are too passive to strike out in holy anger. We are just going to be sitting targets.

Now is the time to strike the ground—to develop aggressiveness in the Spirit. We can become so courageous and so confident in the power and authority that Jesus has given us that we have no fear about the devil attacking us.

Look at these additional words of David from Psalm 18. This great psalm-writing soldier describes the attitude we need:

> Who is God, but the LORD? And who is a rock, except our God[?] . . . He trains my hands for battle, so that my arms can bend a bow of bronze. . . . I pursued my enemies and overtook them, and I did not turn back until they were consumed. I shattered them, so they were not able to rise; they fell under my feet.
>
> Psalm 18:32, 34, 37–38

Jesus is the Lion from the tribe of Judah, and we are His children. We can follow Him into battle with the heart of a warrior. We need to understand the warrior nature of God's Spirit. Exodus 15:3 says: "The LORD is a warrior; the LORD is His name."

I quoted the following verses in chapter 1, but look again at this passage from Revelation.

> And I saw heaven opened, and behold, a white horse, and He who sat on it is called Faithful and True, and in righteousness He judges and wages war. His eyes are a flame of fire, and on His head are many diadems; and He has a name written on Him which no one knows except Himself. He is clothed with a robe dipped in blood, and His name is called The Word of God. And the armies which are in heaven, clothed in fine linen, white and clean, were following Him on white horses.
>
> Revelation 19:11–14

We need to receive the warrior dimension of God's nature and follow Him into battle against darkness with holy violence.

On the Battlefield

Recently I was in Africa preaching the Gospel at a crusade. As I ministered each night, demons that were infesting people began to show themselves. Jesus revealed His glory as I took authority over the demons and released His shalom into these ones who were being set free from the evil spirits.

The last instance of this kind of manifestation was extremely intense. Two of our ushers helped a woman to the platform where I was preaching. She was screaming hysterically; her body was flailing. Her face and head were being thrown back and forth as she continued to shriek. There was literally foam coming out of her mouth.

I took authority over the demons in her in Jesus' name, but she did not seem to be affected by it. After about 45 seconds I had had enough of the antics of these demons. Something rose up in me. I was not going to let this continue. I stepped toward her, clamped my hand over her foamy mouth and, with a holy spiritual anger and resolve, I shouted, "Shut up, Satan!"

Instantly, the demon left. The woman was overcome by the power of the Holy Spirit and fell bodily to the platform basking in His presence. I continued to speak and release the shalom of Jesus over her. She was set free.

Let me sidestep here for a second and say a word about the potential for manifestations of demons as we move forward with spiritual aggression in the process of self-deliverance. Sometimes people are afraid that demons will start speaking through them or take over their bodies when commanded to leave.

Be assured that you do not have to worry. While I have seen demons show themselves through some pretty dramatic sounds or actions in severe cases in Haiti and Africa, as with this woman, it is always true that any manifestation, large or small, is a step toward the freedom of the person they inhabit.

Consider this: If demons show themselves, it is because they are afraid, and know they are about to be evicted. Look at the case in Mark 1:23–25:

> There was a man in their synagogue with an unclean spirit, and he cried out, saying, "What business do we have with each other, Jesus of Nazareth? Have You come to destroy us? I know who You are—the Holy One of God!"

The demons manifested because they were in the presence of God and knew they had to let go of their victim. They were terrified. So do not fear demonic manifestations. They are not doing anything new; they are already present. They are simply being brought to the surface before being evicted. There need be no concern that if you are seeking deliverance you are about to lose control.

Although the process might appear scary to someone who does not understand what is going on, in reality, any demons that manifest are doing so *not because they are gaining control*, but *because they are losing control*. Demons are nothing at King Jesus' feet.

Moving Forward Boldly

Zephaniah 3:17 says that the Lord God, "a victorious warrior," is in our midst. As we take steps forward every day to build our passion to fight for the Kingdom, you and I are going to walk into our inheritance. Here is a prayer to help guide you as you move forward both in perseverance and aggressiveness against the demonic realm.

> *Lord Jesus, thank You for the supernatural impartation I am receiving from You. Thank You for teaching me about persisting against darkness, and doing it with holy violence. Help me, Lord, to love myself enough in You to protect myself from the devil. I want to pursue the enemy ruthlessly, with courage and confidence, just as David did.*
>
> *I ask that Your very presence be imparted to me to help me discern and resist any dark thoughts that are trying to intrude into my mind. When the battle is difficult and I feel weak or ineffective, give me strength to persevere and help me react with holy aggression and spiritual violence against the enemy.*
>
> *Thank You, Holy Spirit, that You are strengthening me in these areas. I look to You and receive. In the holy name of Jesus, Yeshua HaMashiach, Amen.*

9

Facing Reality

John, the beloved disciple, penned words that help us grasp the reality of the universe we are living in. He gave expression to the fact that our experience of life, at its core, is spiritual:

> In the beginning was the Word, and the Word was with God, and the Word was God. He was in the beginning with God. All things came into being through Him, and apart from Him nothing came into being that has come into being. In Him was life, and the life was the Light of men.
>
> John 1:1–4

David echoed the concept of spiritual life and the light that emanates from it when he wrote: "With You is the fountain of life; in Your light we see light" (Psalm 36:9).

There are many types of light in the world. Someone can turn on the light in a room but not necessarily see light.

I remember being depressed when I was eighteen years old, sitting in a beautiful home, looking out the window at beautiful woods. But I did not see any light. It was a lovely environment, but it was not "light" because I did not have God's light.

There are many types of life, as well. Zebras have life. Centipedes have life. Plants have life. There is a kind of energy that drives an organism. But that is not the life we need for Kingdom living.

John was talking about zóé life and zóé light. Zóé means the absolute fullness of life. It comes only from God, and is sustained by Him. This spiritual life and light comes from God and is, in fact, God.

Light and Life Within, Literally

The Bible tells us that God wants us to have His own spiritual life and light inside us. Look once more at these familiar words of Jesus: "Behold, I stand at the door and knock; if anyone hears My voice and opens the door, I will come in" (Revelation 3:20). If we open the doors of our hearts, He actually comes in and takes up residence inside. This means that when we receive Yeshua, we receive a living entity. We receive a living Person: Jesus.

Every believer can move in confidence against demons, because the living God has taken up residence inside.

It follows that whoever has the Son living within also has His zóé life and light. If we believers could go to a supernatural doctor who has supernatural technology and super-natural instruments, the doctor's X rays would show not just the material aspect of the physical body; they would show that the living Spirit of God is actually inside us.

Even common sense tells us that we are more than that which appears to the naked eye. Everything that we see around us is in the process of disintegrating. The natural world is in the process of falling apart, of becoming dust. Even our physical bodies will return to dust. We think they are real, but they are not; they are falling away.

Paul expressed it this way:

Though our outer man is decaying, yet our inner man is being renewed day by day. . . . [We] look not at the things which are seen, but at the things which are not seen; for the things which are seen are temporal, but the things which are not seen are eternal.

2 Corinthians 4:16, 18

Most people are deceived into thinking that the material is what really matters. We need to grasp the fact that the *real* reality for us is not physical. When we start looking at life through the eyes of the Spirit, we enter a whole new realm of freedom. The change that takes place in us when Jesus comes inside through the power of His Spirit is real and tangible. It is scientific reality in the realm of the Spirit. "In Him was life, and the life was the light of men."

We Are Lights in the Darkness

So where is the devil in all of this? In Revelation 2:13, Jesus said to the church in Pergamum: "I know where you dwell, where Satan's throne is." We are living in a world that is surrounded by darkness and decay. But we are lights in this world because the Spirit of the Lord dwells within us.

Look at Jesus' words recorded in the book of Revelation:

> "Do not fear what you are about to suffer. Behold, the devil is about to cast some of you into prison, so that you will be tested, and you will have tribulation for ten days. Be faithful until death, and I will give you the crown of life."
>
> Revelation 2:10

Notice once again from these verses that the devil is roaming the earth seeking to harm God's people. The devil is right here among us. Darkness is here; we simply cannot run from this. But believers in Yeshua do not need to run. We walk in Kingdom victory because of the light and life within us.

The spirit world is the real world. Since we are lights in that world, it does not matter what is going on in the physical realm. The physical is wasting away. In the real world, the true light shines through us. We grow brighter and brighter, and the darkness is diminished. We walk more and more in victory. Acts 26:18 says that Jesus came to open our eyes and turn us "from darkness to light and from the dominion of Satan to God." When we put our faith in Him, Jesus takes us out of the dominion of Satan and into the dominion of God.

I remember a prophetic dream I had some years back. In the dream, I was taken captive by certain men and held hostage by them in a house. Knowing I was about to be tortured, the first thing I did was run all around the house trying to find a way I could escape.

But I came to the conclusion quickly that there was no escape. And when I realized there was no possibility of getting free from these evil men, I turned my attention to facing the reality of the situation.

Once my focus changed, something happened. A powerful spiritual energy welled up within me. It felt like a deep knowing of who I was. When that happened, I had complete peace.

Until I faced the danger, I did not experience peace. When I was running in fear looking for a way out, I was not aware of the power that I had within. It was only when I faced the situation that I felt an undergirding of strength from the Holy Spirit and the reality of God Himself living inside me. It changed everything.

You are a light in the world, and the darkness cannot put you out.

I share that with you because of the obvious parallel to our work of self-deliverance. We need to face reality. We need to look squarely at the nature of the struggle that we are in. When we do, we will have the sense of empowerment that comes from God living within us. The Holy Spirit is always ready to impart to us an extra measure of divine grace so that we can walk in greater Kingdom light and life. We will actually ascend out of the darkness. We move on a trajectory of victory in the cosmic life of Jesus!

We began this chapter by looking at John 1:1–4. Look at the next verse in this section of Scripture. John wrote: "The Light [which is also the life] shines in the darkness, and the darkness did not comprehend it" (John 1:5). Other translations read that the light "did not extinguish it" and "could not overcome it." This confirms for us that the Spirit we have received is the very Spirit of the living God and is a Spirit of absolute victory. This is a Spirit who cannot die. This is eternal life. This is the Holy Spirit, the essence of God Himself.

You know you have the victory because the Spirit of victory is in you. How do you know you win? Because it is already won. You are going to lay hold of it as you press on because God's Spirit is in you.

10

The Shalom of Jesus

We have examined throughout this book the combat zone that we live in, and have learned from God's Word how to be victorious against the demonic powers of darkness that want to destroy us. But, in closing, we need to remember that spiritual warfare is undertaken from our victorious position *in Jesus*. We recall the words of Ephesians 2:6: We have been raised up with Christ Jesus and seated with Him there in the heavenly places. Knowing our identity in Yeshua HaMashiach is our starting point and our ending point. When we dwell in His shalom the enemy cannot touch us.

With that in mind, I want to share with you some verses from Psalm 23 and focus on our peace in Jesus as we face the powers of darkness around us. In this psalm David declared who God was to him and what his relationship with God was like. We have here an opportunity to took into the heart of this man of God—to see what he believed about God and what he experienced in his relationship with God.

Let's pretend that Psalm 23 is brand new to us and ask Jesus to help us receive it at a brand-new level. He can use this beautiful psalm to change us, open us and give us new confidence in Him and all that He wants to do in our lives!

Whenever you find that the fight against the enemy is heating up, or whenever you simply want to know that you are safe and secure within God's care, I want to encourage you to declare this psalm over your life. I hope that these thoughts will help you rest in God's peace.

The Heart of Relationship

The LORD is my shepherd, I shall not want.

It is interesting that in most of the psalms we hear the Lord described in royal or military terms: The Lord is my king; the Lord is my shield; the Lord is my rock.

But here the Lord is described in a very intimate term. Jesus is my shepherd. A shepherd is someone who lives with the sheep. Yeshua is not a starchy monarch who is reigning from a faraway throne. David knew Yeshua as someone who was close to him, who watched over him tenderly, someone who was right with him, just as a shepherd lives with and cares for his flock.

The prophet Isaiah also revealed this same truth about God's intimate nature when he wrote: "Like a shepherd He will tend His flock, in His arm He will gather the lambs and carry them in His bosom; He will gently lead the nursing ewes" (Isaiah 40:11).

When we cling to the Good Shepherd, we have no lack. He lays down His very life for His sheep. And why does He lay down His life for the sheep? So that we can have life, and have it more abundantly.

Also, we need to remind ourselves that whatever the Lord seems to be doing or not doing in other people's lives is not the relevant point here. The verse does not say that the Lord is *their* shepherd. We do not know what another person's relationship with God is really like, or why the things that are happening in other people's lives are happening. If we seek God and cling to Him, we can say like David, "The Lord is *my* shepherd. I shall not want."

He also was confident that "the Lord will accomplish what concerns me" (Psalm 138:8).

Yes, we have a vicious enemy. Yes, there will be tough times. But at the end of the day, we are in the care of a shepherd who loves us. Jesus tells us: "[Nothing] will injure you" (Luke 10:19). He will supply all our needs. We will have His shalom in our hearts and minds. We will not be in a place of fear or lack. He will not let us down. We can boldly say *the Lord is my shepherd.*

Facing Danger Confidently

He makes me lie down in green pastures.

When David wrote this psalm, he was not living on an island or on vacation somewhere. He was not in Acapulco sitting under a tree.

He was facing enemies in what looked like a treacherous place, and yet he was able to say that the Lord "makes me lie down in green pastures." David was able to write this song of confidence at the very moment he was in danger.

We have to face the fact that this world is a dangerous place. Accidents, tragedies, the things we hear on the news about the stock market, the economy, nuclear warfare, countries that hate other countries—danger is all around us. Not only that, but as believers we are doing battle in the spiritual realm, fighting demonic spirits.

How can we have the shalom of Jesus in all of this? We have His peace because He lives in our hearts.

God's peace is present when our thoughts and attitudes are in alignment with His truth. Our attitude can be one of trust and hope in the care of the Good Shepherd, who knows where the green pastures are and makes the way safe for us to lie down there and rest. The battle with evil will not end in our lifetimes, but we can have the strength and wisdom to press our way through to freedom and victory as we rest and are restored by Messiah Jesus and His shalom.

We live in a perilous world just as David did. Like him we have enemies of our spirits, souls and bodies. And yet, even though he was aware of this, David was able to say, "The Lord is taking care of me. I will experience green pastures where I can rest in safety." David knew that God was with him. In Psalm 139:3 David wrote: "You scrutinize my path and my lying down, and are intimately acquainted with all my ways."

This was not an attempt to escape the enemy. This was looking the lion straight in the face and proclaiming that God is greater. We can know that He loves us and is with us. Because of this we are safe. We can *lie down in green pastures.*

Jesus' Power to Restore

He leads me beside quiet waters.

You may know that sheep cannot drink from a river that is moving quickly; they have an adverse reaction to that. Sheep will drink only when the water is still. David was telling us in these words that just as the shepherd leads his sheep to still waters that they can drink from, so, too, the Lord knew what type of water he could drink. He was leading David to that particular supply. The Lord knows what we need and how we can receive it.

Each one of us is at a different place in our lives. Each one of us is able to feed on different things in different seasons. I think back in my life and look at some of the places where God fed me in those early days. You could say that I was not far along the road of sanctification, and you would be right! But Yeshua met me there and gave me water I could drink, so that I could be refreshed and keep walking.

In those beginning days of my walk with Yeshua, before Cynthia and I were married, I shared the Gospel with her, and she received the Lord. She told me later that if I had come to her all clean-cut and polished and with all the right words to say, she would not have been able to identify with me and receive the Gospel message. She would have found it hard to see Jesus. The Lord met her in "*quiet* waters"—in other words, in waters that she could receive from.

This is a beautiful thing. The Lord loves us intimately. He knows exactly the type of food that we are capable of eating, and the type of stream that we are capable of drinking from. He knows what it is going to take for us to be able to ingest Him, you could say. And He feeds us that way. He feeds one person one way, another person another way, another person yet another way. He knows what you need and what I need, and *He leads us beside quiet waters.*

God Hears and Answers

He restores my soul.

One morning not long ago I woke up and did not feel good. I had been under a lot of pressure and maybe that had something to do with it. I prayed during my devotional time, but had no peace, no shalom. I felt as though my mind was scattered.

So I prayed this: "Lord, I really need You. Please bring restoration and renewal to me today."

And you know what? A little past half the day I felt refreshed. I felt brand new. God had restored my soul. When I brought my need to Him, He responded by pouring His shalom into my burdened and anxious mind.

We are going to be wounded in life at times, grieved, pained, under stress and pressure. Things will happen from the realm of darkness that we cannot understand. But we have a God who cares. As we look to Him, we are renewed day by day. *He restores my soul.*

Doing What Is "Right"

He guides me in the paths of righteousness.

A lot of times we hear the word *righteous*, and we do not know how to relate to it. We know that God is righteous, that He is morally impeccable—*impeccable* means "perfect." But how do we relate to that? How can we be righteous? Even when we know that it is only in Jesus that we are righteous, we still know who we are when we look into the mirror and see the good, the bad and the ugly.

We need to rethink what it means to be righteous. Righteousness is not only moral perfection or impeccability. Righteousness simply means being rightly related to God, and choosing and doing what is right. So when you and I read here that Jesus guides us in the paths of righteousness, it means that He guides us in the path that is right. This means so much more than we may realize.

As a simple illustration, suppose you are going to buy a new car. There are a million salesmen out there who are vying for your business—and some of them will try to take advantage of you. God wants to lead you on the path to the car that is best for you. He will help you choose what is right—and often only He knows what is right. Suppose, for example, you see about fourteen cars that you really like. Only God knows which one is going to last the longest and require the least maintenance. He will lead you in the right path. He will guide you to make the right decision.

Can you imagine what would happen to us if we did not have a God who goes before us, leading us? This is why it is so important that we cling to Him. Remember the words that God spoke to me, telling me that many are hurting because they are not clinging to Him. He was saying, *If they would cling to Me, I would lead them to make the right decisions, to think the right thoughts, to have the right relationships and to choose the right way. And they would experience an abundant life.*

What a blessing! That is shalom living.

To remain in God's shalom, we need not to rely on our own confidence. If we think that we can rely on our own intuition or reasoning powers alone, then we are going to have a hard time following Him on the right path. If we are living out of the soul, then we are living out of the "self" and will not experience God in an abundant way.

Thanks to Jesus, there is a way out. There is a way into victory. It does not matter how broken we are or how much we have failed in the past. There is a way up, and there is a way out. Jesus is that way. He leads you and me in the right path.

Close to twenty years ago I was getting ready to make a move. I did not know what to do next with my life. One night I was asleep, and I had a vision. It lasted only a second. Above my head I saw a rainbow-colored halo. Inside the halo was the word *Columbus*.

I knew this referred to Columbus, Ohio, but I knew next to nothing about Columbus, Ohio. I had no close friends in Columbus. I was not thinking about Columbus. But you know what? As a result of that vision, our family moved to Columbus. We recognized that it was the Holy Spirit's leading. And ever since I followed that path, I have been blessed.

What would have happened if I had moved someplace else? What if I had moved to New York or Arkansas? I would have missed the right path. Sometimes we are going to miss the path. Sometimes we stray as sheep often do. But if we repent, the Good Shepherd will lead us back. He is a big God. He knows how to find us. And it is not as though He cannot bless us wherever we are. If we cling to Jesus, even if we miss the way, He knows the path that will guide us back into His will. He guides us in *the paths of righteousness.*

We Honor Him

For His name's sake.

He "guides me in the paths of righteousness." Why? Because He loves me. Yes! But He also does this "for His name's sake."

Jesus loves you and me. Immensely. He guides us, helps us, feeds us, restores us.

But even greater than this reality is the honor of His own name. We have been saved "to the praise of the glory of His grace" (Ephesians 1:6). We have been chosen as vessels of mercy so that He will be glorified as we freely praise Him forever and ever.

He chose to love us, and now He blesses us. He wants His glory to be manifested in our lives (see Ephesians 1:1–12) *for His name's sake.*

Having No Fear

Even though I walk through the valley of the shadow of death, I fear no evil, for You are with me.

Notice again that David was not looking at some far-away danger. He was not anticipating something lurking out in the distance. No, he was in the midst of the battle. He was at war right when he wrote this. He said, "I walk *through* the valley of the shadow of death." He was walking through the valley as he wrote those words.

And what was his mentality in this dangerous time? He had no fear of evil. In the midst of the battle he had triumph. He had a spirit and attitude of victory.

I am human just like you, and there are times that I am not living as though I believe the Good Shepherd is truly with me. I know this because of what I am thinking. When I am overcome by thoughts of anxiety or fear, getting caught up in all the details and getting anxious, I am not trusting that He is with me.

Our thoughts are an important reality check. We can *say* that we believe He is with us, but the test is where the rubber meets the road. What do we think when we face demonic spirits of fear that threaten to stop us or undo us? Do we believe at those times that He is with us? That we can move through our valleys in the shadow of death? Do we stay in confidence?

Monitoring the thoughts that are going through our heads needs to be a daily thing. If we begin to feel separation from God, any fearfulness, any sense of being lost, we need to say, "Father God, help me really believe that You are with me—that You love me, that You're covering me, that You're leading me, that You're going to bless me, that You're guiding me. Father God, help me to understand Your love in a deeper way. Help me to know that You are with me. Help me to know that I do not need to be afraid in this valley of the shadow of death. I believe that You are working everything that I am going through for Your good and for my good, and that Your blessing is upon me."

When we hold that confidence, the fear is going to be broken under our feet. Instead of that mountain looming over us, looking bigger than we are, we are going to know that it is under us. We will be able to say, like David, *even though I walk through the valley of the shadow of death, I fear no evil, for You are with me.*

The God of All Comfort

Your rod and Your staff, they comfort me.

A rod in David's day was like a club. It was used to break the enemy. The Good Shepherd's rod, His club, gives us protection, and we can take great comfort in that. He uses it to break the powers of the enemy off us.

The staff, on the other hand, was for disciplining the sheep, to keep them plodding along the right path. Sheep—everybody knows this—really need a shepherd. Without a shepherd, sheep get lost. They have no way to find water. They are very vulnerable creatures. The staff, then, shows that the Lord disciplines everyone He receives.

I find great comfort in this—knowing that it is not up to me to get it right every single time. I can stay on the right path because I have a shepherd who disciplines me with His staff.

Hebrews 12 says this:

"My son, do not regard lightly the discipline of the Lord, nor faint when you are reproved by Him." . . . God deals with you as with sons; for what son is there whom his father does not discipline? . . . [Fathers] disciplined us for a short time as seemed best to them, but He disciplines us for our good, so that we may share His holiness. . . . To those who have been trained by [discipline], afterwards it yields the peaceful fruit of righteousness.

verses 5, 7, 10–11

Jesus tells us plainly that we are like sheep without a shepherd. We cannot make it on our own. David knew this and took comfort in the fact that the Father's rod was clubbing his enemy, and that His staff was guiding him. *Your rod and Your staff, they comfort me.*

Blessing—Even During Attack

You prepare a table before me in the presence of my enemies.

If we believe and know, even in the midst of demonic attack, that God is going to be blessing us and giving us victory, we will walk in deep peace. Many of us have experienced this. We find ourselves right in the middle of something that in the natural we might be afraid of—but in that situation, we experience the shalom of the Lord.

I remember talking to somebody not long ago who had just lost his job. For months before this happened, there was talk of downsizing his company. He grew terrified that it might happen to him. It was causing him constant anxiety. Then, finally, it happened. He was called into the boss's office and was let go—and you know what? He was not afraid but had peace! The presence of the Lord was with him. He was seated at a bountiful table even in the presence of seeming lack.

The devil's cheap tool is fear. God wants us to have confidence that when bad things happen in life, He will be there in the midst of that danger, in the midst of that difficulty, in the midst of that assault. He will be there, and we are going to be blessed in the midst of it! Praise God! Let's believe God and break off the power of the enemy.

Notice also that David specified the valley of the *shadow* of death. Can a shadow hurt you? No. It is just a phantom. For God's people, all our fears, even the fear of death itself, is just a shadow. "O death, where is your victory? O death, where is your sting?" (1 Corinthians 15:55). I will not be afraid, even in *the presence of my enemies*.

Receive and Then Give

You have anointed my head with oil; my cup overflows.

Look at how much of God's shalom He pours out on us: Our cup runs over so that we have enough for ourselves and enough to share. We have a God who is abundant and who wants us to trust Him to experience an abundant life. To experience His abundance we have to cooperate with Him by being givers.

When we are blessed and give to others, we open a channel for God, who is by nature a giving God, to flow into us and through us in an even greater way. Jesus said, "Give, and it will be given to you. They will pour into your lap a good measure—pressed down, shaken together, and running over" (Luke 6:38).

We *give*! We go out of our way to reach out to people, to bless people, to encourage people, to tell people we love them.

There are going to be some people we do not feel like loving, some people we do not feel like reaching out to, some people we do not feel like being in relationship with. But you know what? We force ourselves to reach out, to give, to be messengers and couriers of love. And when we do, the anointing is released. Giving to others opens a huge portal over our lives for heaven to flow down onto us from above. *Our cup of shalom overflows.*

Time to Trust

Surely goodness and lovingkindness will follow me all the days of my life, and I will dwell in the house of the LORD forever.

God wants you to be confident that you are blessed! In Jesus you will always be blessed, all the days of your life. In fact, this verse is saying that God's mercy and blessing on your life are actually pursuing you. They are not just following you or flowing toward you from a distance; they are overtaking you. And in Jesus it will always be this way. In Him, it is done.

It is very important to believe this, because when you can look into the future with confidence, the devil will not be able to put his fear in you. If we refuse to face the future with a spirit of doom, whereby we expect something bad to happen, but rather believe that we are blessed, we can wake each day in happiness looking into His face.

When we are confident, the devil is broken off. As we look into the future with assurance rather than foreboding, we are going to be blessed.

God's goodness and mercy will pursue us. This is our state. We are blessed today and tomorrow. There is nothing to fear. That is how we gain victory over the powers of darkness and walk in freedom every day of our lives—by believing and being confident in God!

The Good Road Ahead

Overcoming darkness is a progressive journey. Every season you are going to climb higher and higher. And as you go higher, the climb gets easier. You will have more light, more vision, more confidence and more knowledge of how to use the weapons of warfare for self-deliverance and Kingdom living. Then when you get to the end of your life, you are going to turn and look back down the mountain and see how high you have come!

You will overcome the darkness, and the darkness will never overcome you.

Study Questions

Chapter 1: The Battle Begins

1. Many people find it difficult to believe that demons are real—or that they are a real threat to believers. What would you say to someone who accepts the fact that demons existed in Jesus' day, but considers them irrelevant to the present-day Church?

2. Is it unsettling to consider that demons might be "squatters" in your own heart and mind? What change does it make to realize that any spiritual squatters camped in you are there illegally—and can be driven out?

3. Do you have fear of being "possessed" by demons? Where did that fear originate?

4. The children of Israel had to "drive out" the inhabitants of their Promised Land. Does this story help you

understand the spiritual battle with demons? Why or why not?

5. If you are truly in a spiritual battle with a spiritual enemy, do the words "Our God is a God of war" give you insight into His plans for your freedom? (See Exodus 15:3; Psalm 144:1; Revelation 19:11–16.)

Chapter 2: How Demons Gain Access

1. Revelation 12 describes Satan, the "serpent of old," being cast out of heaven along with his angels. What does this tell you about demons, their personalities and their motives?

2. If you struggle in a certain area, and cannot seem to break free, are you willing to ask God to show you the truth about any demonic activity that may be keeping you from walking in victory? Why or why not?

3. The Bible speaks of generational curses and blessings. What evidence of both do you see in your family line? Are any "familiar spirits" affecting you?

4. Sin swings the door wide open to demonic bondage. What do you think would happen if you asked God to show you any area of sin hidden in your own life?

5. Wounding from others is a significant opening for demons. Are there areas of hurt that have caused you fear, doubt or self-defeat? Can you believe that Jesus wants you to know His peace in that area?

Chapter 3: Three Steps to Closing the Door

1. After reading this teaching about confession, did you sense that there were weaknesses in your life—behaviors, attitudes, actions or thoughts—that you wanted to surrender to Jesus? What was the outcome?

2. If the Holy Spirit brought to your awareness an area in your life or your family line to confess before Him, you are ready for the next step: to repent. What does *repentance* mean in the battle against demons? What are some examples you have seen of the difference repentance can make?

3. How is unforgiveness an opening for demons?

4. What is the hardest thing you can imagine forgiving someone for? Is it harder to forgive someone else for a wrong done to you, or to forgive yourself for the wrongs you have done?

5. These three steps of confessing, repenting and forgiving can effectively cancel the rights of demons to torment you and close the door on them. Do you feel encouraged to press on to the specific aspects of self-deliverance? Why or why not?

Chapter 4: Stand in Authority, Move in Power

1. What does it mean in the study of self-deliverance that "when your blade's sharp, you don't have to cut so hard"?

2. Do you think demons must obey someone who stands in Jesus' authority and moves in His power? What does that mean for you personally? Do you feel you are growing in one or both of these areas?

3. What do Paul's words "When I am weak, then I am strong" mean to you?

4. Considering the importance of relationship with Jesus in the area of deliverance, how would you summarize in one sentence the sorry outcome of the sons of Sceva?

5. Have you considered that the same power that raised Jesus from the dead is inside every believer—including you? What difference could that knowledge make in your life?

6. What is one area in which you want to realize your authority over demonic oppression? What is one area where you want to grow in power over demonic oppression?

Chapter 5: Should We Speak to Demons?

1. What was your position about addressing demons before reading this chapter?

2. What do you learn from Jesus' examples of addressing demons that you can apply to your own life?

3. If you think about your own battle against darkness, what difficulties stand out as harassment from demons? How can you tell?

4. Consider the four steps of self-deliverance: (1) Identify the presence of a demon; (2) Command the spirit to go; (3) Confess the positive; (4) Be aware that demons will try to return. Did you find these steps difficult to do, or were you eager to proceed? What does that tell you about growing in your position of authority and power in Jesus? In what ways are you encouraged?

5. How can you stand firm in what was accomplished through this deliverance process, even if it seems as though "nothing has changed"?

Chapter 6: Keeping Control of Your Thoughts

1. Do you remember a time when you were deceived by a thought that likely came from a demon? How was your perspective warped by that thought?

2. What are some words in Scripture that underscore the kinds of thoughts that come from God, the kinds of thoughts that come from the enemy and the kinds of thoughts that come from the flesh? (See Philippians 4:8; Colossians 3:2, 5–6, 8.) What are examples of this in your own experience?

3. One simple command can send demons running when they try to impress lies into your mind. It is this: "I reject you, Satan. Get out of my head!" What do you think will be the most difficult part of taking this stand against the evil coming at you: Is it recognizing the lie that is traveling through your head; speaking

the command; or persisting when the lie enters your thoughts again and again?

4. Which verse in Scripture gives you the most encouragement to stand firm in this battle? Write it down and put it in a place where you will see it often as you press in, press on and fight to win.

Chapter 7: When the Going Gets Rough

1. What causes you the most doubt about staying the course and walking in freedom from demonic harassment?

2. Sometimes the Lord leads His people to fast and pray in order to move particular mountains in their lives. If you have had an experience with fasting, what impact did it have (or not have) on the mountain you were trying to move? If you have never fasted, think about why not.

3. What does fasting say about denying the flesh? About hungering for the Spirit?

4. What does "pray without ceasing" mean to you? How is constant communion with Jesus possible? Why is this important in self-deliverance warfare?

Chapter 8: The Violent Take the Kingdom

1. Have you ever considered "holy violence" as a part of your weaponry against demons? Why might aggression seem out of place in spiritual matters?

2. Do you have trouble picturing Jesus as both the "Prince of peace" and the "destroyer" of the works of the devil? Why or why not?

3. God gave Israel the Promised Land, but His people still had to fight a strong enemy in order to take possession and live there freely. What would help you develop a similar spiritual resolve against darkness in your own battle for freedom?

4. How do you determine when to take the sword up and when to put the sword away (see Luke 22:36; John 18:11)? Who is the real target?

5. How do you respond when you read that God told Israel to "utterly destroy" her enemies in the Promised Land? Can you extend this concept to your own aggression against darkness? Why or why not?

Chapter 9: Facing Reality

1. If you could go to a supernatural doctor who had a supernatural X-ray machine that could show Jesus actually residing in your heart, would you go?

2. What difference do you think it would make in your battle against demons to know, without doubt, that the Son of God, with His fullness of light and life, lives within you?

3. Believers in Yeshua have His light and life within. Do you see yourself as a light in a spiritually dark world? How can you walk in greater Kingdom light and life?

4. The Spirit of God living within you is a Spirit of absolute victory. How can you encourage yourself and others with that truth?

Chapter 10: The Shalom of Jesus

1. Self-deliverance takes place from a victorious position in Jesus. In what ways has your vantage point changed as you have learned these principles of self-deliverance?

2. Which particular line from Psalm 23, in this study of Yeshua's peace, touched you most deeply? Why?

3. What does it mean for you that Jesus is the Good Shepherd and that you are one of His sheep? Do these areas of His protective care seem real as you stand in battle with the enemy?

4. David understood the perilous life of someone with a strong enemy. How can you maintain an attitude of trust in the One who says that He walks alongside you—in both beautiful meadows and dark valleys?

5. How do you live in Jesus' peace, as you learn to walk in freedom from darkness every day of your life?

In 1978, having no concept of or familiarity with Jesus, feeling isolated, unfulfilled and lost, a young Jewish man was suddenly awakened from his sleep. Immediately, a vision appeared to him of Jesus on the cross. "I knew at that instant that Jesus was the answer I had been searching for," says **Messianic Rabbi K. A. Schneider.**

For the first time, he began reading the New Testament, devouring every verse; he says it was like fire to him. He became consumed with knowing and experiencing God, the revelation of His Word and the glory of His Son.

During the past thirty years, Rabbi Schneider has committed his life to a passionate pursuit of Jesus and to being used by God for His glory. Through his years of experience in both personal spiritual warfare and ministry, Rabbi Schneider is able to bring to God's Church deep insight into how to gain victory over Satan and the realm of darkness.

Today Rabbi Schneider hosts the powerful television show *Discovering the Jewish Jesus*, which is available seven days a week in more than one hundred million homes in the United States and approximately two hundred nations worldwide. Viewers tune in regularly as Rabbi Schneider brings revelation on how the Old and New Testaments are integrated, building faith and changing lives.

Several years ago God told Rabbi Schneider, *You are an evangelist*. The fulfillment of this calling is now being witnessed by thousands who attend his crusades across Africa. Preaching to large crowds, Rabbi Schneider has seen the truths of God's Word confirmed by the Holy Spirit, with signs and wonders of healings and deliverance.

Rabbi Schneider leads the congregation Lion of Judah World Outreach Center in Toledo, Ohio. He has authored two previous books, *Awakening to Messiah* and *Do Not Be Afraid*. He is a frequent guest on several Christian television programs, including TBN's *Praise the Lord* and Daystar's *Marcus and Joni*. He and his wife, Cynthia, have two children and live near Columbus, Ohio.

For more information, please visit his website, Discovering TheJewishJesus.com.